AN INTRODUCTION TO
THE ENGLISH NOVEL

VOLUME II

English Literature

Editor

PROFESSOR JOHN LAWLOR
MA

Professor of English Language and
Literature in the University of Keele

By the same author

An Introduction to the English Novel
VOLUME I: TO GEORGE ELIOT

AN INTRODUCTION TO
THE ENGLISH NOVEL

VOLUME II
HENRY JAMES TO 1950

Arnold Kettle

Professor of Literature at the Open
University, Milton Keynes

HUTCHINSON
London Melbourne Sydney Auckland Johannesburg

Hutchinson & Co. (Publishers) Ltd

An imprint of the Hutchinson Publishing Group

17–21 Conway Street, London WIP 5HL

Hutchinson Group (Australia) Pty Ltd
30–32 Cremorne Street, Richmond South, Victoria 3121
PO Box 151, Broadway, New South Wales 2007

Hutchinson Group (NZ) Ltd
32–34 View Road, PO Box 40–086, Glenfield, Auckland 10

Hutchinson Group (SA) (Pty) Ltd
PO Box 337, Bergvlei 2012, South Africa

First published 1953
Reprinted 1955, 1957, 1959,
1961, 1962, 1965
Second edition 1967
Reprinted 1969, 1972, 1974, 1976, 1978, 1981

Printed in Great Britain by litho by The Anchor Press Ltd
and bound by Wm Brendon & Son Ltd
both of Tiptree, Essex

ISBN 0 09 048544 0

CONTENTS

PART III: THE TWENTIETH CENTURY—
THE SECOND QUARTER

PREFACE

As in the first volume of this little work, I have eschewed comprehensiveness in favour of concentration on a few specific books. My object has been to build a discussion of the development of the modern English novel around the study of a dozen or so novels which have, in their different ways, a more than casual significance. One of the problems of the student of the novel, whether he is the individual 'reader for pleasure' or the member of some kind of educational group, is that novels are often rather long and the discussion of them vaguer than it need be. By concentrating on a few books I have hoped to provide a manageable syllabus for, say, a year or so's reading. Books of criticism which are not read in conjunction with the work they are discussing nearly always do more harm than good.

In venturing to write about contemporary and near-contemporary literature one is obviously laying oneself open to all kinds of difficulties. I make no claim whatever to have given each of the novels I have discussed its correct proportion of space or its ultimate evaluation, though naturally I have tried to concentrate on what seems to me most worth while. I have no doubt at all that I have missed out completely a number of books and writers more worthy of consideration than some I have touched on. Nor do I doubt that some of my judgements will look silly even to myself should I live another forty years.

I should like once again to thank the friends who in advice and conversation have given me help, and to express my gratitude to the following individuals and publishing houses for their permission to make numerous quotations:

John Farquharson, on behalf of the estate of the late Henry
James (for passages from *The Portrait of a Lady*); Messrs Mac-
millan & Co (*Tess of the D'Urbervilles*); The Hogarth Press Ltd
(quotations from Virginia Woolf's works and *Party Going*); Mrs
Frieda Lawrence; Messrs Edward Arnold & Co (*A Passage to
India*); Mr Graham Greene; Miss Ivy Compton-Burnett and Messrs
Eyre & Spottiswoode (*A Family and a Fortune*); Mr Joyce Cary
and Messrs Michael Joseph (*Mister Johnson*); and Mr Henry
Green.

1953   A.K.

PART I
The Last Victorians

I

INTRODUCTION

The end of one epoch is the beginning of another. The three novels with the examination of which this volume opens do not look backwards. Each of these writers—Henry James, Butler, Hardy—is very much of his time; but if one calls them the last Victorians it is not to indicate a mere obstinate clinging to a passing world. There is more than a whiff of the future in their work.

The late Victorian period marks the beginning of the disintegration of the epoch ushered in a century before by the Industrial Revolution, the epoch in which Britain became the workshop and the banker of the world. After about 1870 the apparently secure foundations of the world of the London and Manchester business men began to be shaken. It was not until the outbreak of the First World War in 1914 that the full horror became clear, but by then for nearly half a century the process of disintegration had been going on. The late Victorian period may still seem to us superficially, as we look back on it, an era of stability, of the respectable elderly queen, of stuffy clothes and heavy architecture, of comfortable middle-class incomes from the Stock Exchange, of the English Sunday and the gradual extension of the franchise and of free education. But it was also an era of desperation—of a hectic and bloody imperial race against new upstart competitors, of the first modern economic slump, of the rise of the Labour movement as we know it, of the dock strike and Bloody Sunday, of the impact of Darwin and T. H. Huxley, of William Morris and Bernard Shaw (to say nothing of Ibsen and Tolstoy and Marx), of the aesthetes and the *Yellow Book*, of Charles Bradlaugh and Beatrice Webb.

In Samuel Butler and Thomas Hardy it is quite clearly the latter aspect of the age—the opposite of stability—that we find most strikingly expressed. They are, even to a casual glance, novelists of the disintegration, rebels and critics, crying out (sometimes, it seems to the sophisticated middle-class reader, a bit too shrilly) against the sanctities and ethics of the Victorian bourgeois world. Butler is very much a part of that world and this fact, as we shall see, has its effect on his writing. Hardy, the countryman, soaked in the older, pre-capitalist culture of peasant Wessex, is less involved in the values he is attacking and achieves in his two final novels, *Tess* and *Jude*, tragedy which—for all the limitations we shall have to examine—bitterly and poignantly captures a central truth of the era in which he lived.

Henry James is perhaps less obviously a novelist of the disintegration. The social aura that surrounds both the man and his work is that of the well-to-do Victorian middle class, leisured, well-fed, moving securely if not always elegantly through a scene cluttered up with bric-à-brac and *objets d'art*. But to see James merely as the rather snobbish sharer in such a world is to emphasise what is least important in a great novelist. James, it is true, was a bourgeois writer, the bourgeois novelist, one might say, at his most exquisite, most refined point. But his work, like that of Balzac—with whom he has more in common than a hasty estimate might allow—subtly transcends in much of its effect the ideas and the values which appear to infect it at its roots. There *is*, as we shall see, something wrong at the very heart of James the novelist. Yet this does not permit us to undervalue him. No novelist has explored with quite so fine, nor quite so disciplined an art the ramifications of the complex consciousness of latter-day bourgeois man. To read James uncritically or exclusively is, of course, fatal; but to read him with the kind of insight he deserves is to penetrate deep into the spiritual situation involved in the disintegration of the bourgeois world.

That James himself was at an obscure and impressive level of experience aware of this disintegration is revealed by implication in the remarkable novel *The Princess Casamassima* and then clearly as in a flash in the letter he wrote* at that most symbolic of moments —the outbreak of the First World War. In the last two years of his life he drew back from the exploration of this vision; but that he had had a glimpse of it is a measure of the quality of his perception.

These novelists of the late Victorian age are not technically, any

* Quoted Vol. I, p. 85.

more than socially, revolutionaries; but each of them had something new to say and therefore had to discover new means of expression, new ways of modifying or transforming existing techniques to meet new needs. With Butler and Hardy technical preoccupation is on a far lower level than with James. They are content, essentially, to stretch old forms a little in order to receive a new content. Butler, typically, looks back to the eighteenth century; he gets rid of the Dickensian plot along with the Dickensian poetry and other 'literary garbage'. His analytical method, his consistent object of debunking humbug and pretension, together with his rather limited positive sense of human development, lead him to employ for his novel what is fundamentally the technique of *Joseph Andrews* or *Vanity Fair*, though his range is narrower, his control a good deal tighter and his view of life more incisive than is the case with either Fielding or Thackeray.

Hardy, for his part, uses and only slightly modifies the conventional nineteenth-century novel structure. His work is in the tradition of the English moral fable—of *Hard Times* and *North and South* and *Silas Marner*.

James is, in a far more striking degree, an innovator. His aim, as we shall see, is the exploration, in terms more subtle than any before attempted, of the furthest reaches of the refined consciousness. Hence his immense interest in presentation, his peculiar development of prose style (the inability in his last novels ever to resist that last, even more finely modulated qualification) and also his link with the immediate future development of the novel.

It is James rather than Butler and Hardy—for all their self-conscious modernity of theme and outlook—who is the principal signpost towards what we have come to think of as the characteristically 'modern' experiments of the early twentieth-century novel, towards—different as they are—Proust and Joyce and Virginia Woolf. Whether we are to regard this historical position as a strengthening of James's claims to greatness will depend, of course, on whether we finally assess the trend of which his work is a part as a healthy and hopeful one or rather as a dead end, a withered branch,* of the main developing tradition of English fiction. It is one of the purposes of this little book to discuss this very question.

* See D. S. Savage: *The Withered Branch, Six Studies in the Modern Novel* (1950).

2

HENRY JAMES: THE PORTRAIT OF A LADY
(1880–81)

Compared with this the English novels which precede it, except perhaps those of Jane Austen, all seem a trifle crude. There is a habit of perfection here, a certainty and a poise, which is quite different from the merits and power of *Oliver Twist* or *Wuthering Heights* or even *Middlemarch*. The quality has something to do with the full consciousness of Henry James's art. Nothing in *The Portrait of a Lady* is unconscious, nothing there by chance, no ungathered wayward strands, no clumsiness. No novelist is so absorbed as James in what he himself might call his 'game'. But it is not an empty or superficial concern with 'form' that gives *The Portrait of a Lady* its quality. James's manner, his obsession with style, his intricate and passionate concern with presentation, do not spring from a narrow 'aesthetic' attitude to his art.

James had in his style and perhaps in the life which it reflected an idiosyncrasy so powerful, so overwhelming, that to many it seemed a stultifying vice, or at least an inexcusable heresy. . . . He enjoyed an excess of intelligence and he suffered, both in life and art, from an excessive effort to communicate it, to represent it in all its fullness. His style grew elaborate in the degree that he rendered shades and refinements of meaning and feeling not usually rendered at all. . . . His intention and all his labour was to represent dramatically intelligence at its most difficult, its most lucid, its most beautiful point. This is the sum of his idiosyncrasy.[1]

The Portrait of a Lady is not one of James's 'difficult' novels; but

---

[1] Superior figures refer to Notes and References, pp. 179–183.

Mr Blackmur's remarks usefully remind us of the inadequacy of a
merely formal approach to James's work. The extraordinary richness of texture of his novels makes such an approach tempting; but
it will take us neither to James's triumphs nor to his failures.

The beauty of texture derives immediately from two qualities,
which are ultimately inseparable. One is James's ability to make us
know his characters more richly, though not necessarily more
vividly, than we know the characters of other novelists; the other
is the subtlety of his own standpoint. Without the latter quality the
former would not, of course, be possible. You cannot control the
responses of your reader unless you are in complete control of your
material.

In *The Portrait of a Lady* there are—looking at the question
from an analytical point of view—two kinds of characters: those
whom we know from straightforward, though not unsubtle, description by the author and those who reveal themselves in the
course of the book. The latter are, obviously, the important ones.
The former—Mrs Touchett, Henrietta Stackpole, the Countess
Gemini, Pansy Osmond—are interesting primarily in their relationship to the chief characters, in their part in the pattern; we do not
follow their existence out of their function in the book. But they are
nevertheless not 'flat' characters. They come alive not as 'characters', not as personified 'humours', but as complete people (Pansy,
perhaps, is the exception, but then is it not the intention that we
should see her as scarcely an independent being at all?) and if we do
not follow them out of the part of the plot which concerns them it
is because our interests are more involved elsewhere, not because
they do not have a full existence of their own.

The way Henry James introduces his characters to us depends
entirely on the kind of function they are to have in his story. The
main characters are never described as they *are* (i.e. as the author
knows them to be) but—by and large—as Isabel Archer sees them.
We know them at first only by the first impression that they make.
We get to know better what they are like in the way that, in life, we
get to know people better through acquaintance. And just as in life
we are seldom, if ever, quite certain what another person is like, so
in a Henry James novel we are often pretty much at sea about
particular characters for considerable portions of the book. In *The
Portrait of a Lady* the person whom at first we inevitably know
least about is Madame Merle. Henry James lets us know right from
the start that there is something sinister about her; we are made
quickly to feel that Isabel's reaction to her is less than adequate,

but the precise nature of her character is not revealed until fairly far into the book.

It is not quite true to say that everything in *The Portrait of a Lady* is revealed through Isabel's consciousness. We know, from the start, certain things that Isabel does not know. We know, for instance—and twice Henry James explicitly reminds us of it—more about Ralph Touchett's feeling for Isabel than she herself perceives.

Indeed, there is a sense in which the novel is revealed to us through Ralph's consciousness, for his is the 'finest', the fullest intelligence in the book and therefore he sees things—about Madame Merle, about Osmond, about Isabel herself—which Isabel does not see and inevitably such perceptions are transmitted to the reader. Again, we are offered important scenes—between Madame Merle and Osmond, between the Countess and Madame Merle— which reveal to us not the whole truth but enough of the truth about Madame Merle's stratagems to put us at an advantage over Isabel.

The truth is that Henry James's purpose in this novel is not to put Isabel between the reader and the situation (in the way that Strether's consciousness is used in *The Ambassadors*) but to reveal to the reader the full implications of Isabel's consciousness. For this to happen we must see Isabel not merely from the inside (i.e. know how she feels) but from the outside too. The method is, in fact, precisely the method of *Emma*, except that Jane Austen is rather more scrupulously consistent than Henry James. The scenes 'outside' Emma herself (like Jane Fairfax's visits to the post office) are brought to our knowledge by being related by a third party in the presence of Emma herself. Our only 'advantage' over Emma herself is provided by the words which Jane Austen uses to describe her. Henry James, as we have seen, takes greater liberties. Yet it is worth observing that the great scene at the centre of *The Portrait of a Lady* (ch. XIII), in which Isabel takes stock of her situation, is of precisely the same *kind* as the scene in which (Vol. I, ch. XVI) Emma takes stock of her dealings with Harriet.

Since James's purpose is to render the full implications of Isabel's situation it is necessary that we should know more than Isabel, should see her, that is to say, from the outside. The question remains how *much* more should we know? And James's answer is: just as much as is necessary for a fully sympathetic understanding. Thus we are to know that Madame Merle has drawn Isabel into a trap, but we are not to know why. The full story is kept back, not because Henry James is interested in suspense in the melodramatic sense, but because if we were in on the secret the nature of Isabel's discovery of her situation could not be so effectively revealed. It is necessary to the novel that we should *share* Isabel's suspicions and her awakening. In order to give the precise weight (not just the logical weight but the intricate weight of feelings, standards, loyalties) to the issues involved in her final dilemma we must know not just what has happened to Isabel but the way it has happened.

It is from such a consideration that there will emerge one of Henry James's cardinal contributions to the art of the novel. With James the question 'What happened?' carries the most subtle, the most exciting ramifications. To no previous novelist had the answer to such a question seemed so difficult, its implications so interminable. To a George Eliot the question is complicated enough: to understand what happened to Lydgate we must be made aware of innumerable issues, facets of character, moral choices, social pressures. And yet deep in George Eliot's novel is implicit the idea that if the reader only knows enough facts about the situation he will know the situation. It is the aim of Henry James to avoid the 'about' or, at least, to alter its status, to transform quantity into quality. His is the poet's ambition: to create an object about which we say not 'It means. . . .' but 'It is. . . .' (In this he is with Emily Brontë.) We cannot *understand* Isabel Archer, he implies, unless we feel as she feels. And it is, indeed, because he succeeds in this attempt that *The Portrait of a Lady* though not a greater novel than *Middlemarch* is a more moving one.

As a rule when Henry James describes a character (as opposed to allowing the person to be revealed in action) the description is of the kind we have noticed in *Emma* or *Middlemarch*.

Mrs Touchett was certainly a person of many oddities, of which her behaviour on returning to her husband's house after many months was a noticeable specimen. She had her own way of doing all that she did, and this is the simplest description of a character which, although by no means without liberal motions, rarely succeeded in giving an impression of suavity. Mrs Touchett might do a great deal of good, but she never pleased. This way of her own, of which she was so fond, was not intrinsically offensive—it was just unmistakeably distinguished from the way of others. The edges of her conduct were so very clear-cut that for susceptible persons it sometimes had a knife-like effect. That hard fineness came out in her deportment during the first hours of her return from America, under circumstances in which it might have seemed that her first act would have been to exchange greetings with her husband and son. Mrs Touchett, for reasons which she deemed excellent, always retired on such occasions into impenetrable seclusion, postponing the

more sentimental ceremony until she had repaired the disorder of dress
with a completeness which had the less reason to be of high importance
as neither beauty nor vanity were concerned in it. She was a plain-faced
old woman, without graces and without any great elegance, but with an
extreme respect for her own motives. She was usually prepared to explain
these—when the explanation was asked as a favour; and in such a case
they proved totally different from those that had been attributed to her.
She was virtually separated from her husband, but she appeared to perceive nothing irregular in the situation. It had become clear, at an early
stage of their community, that they should never desire the same thing
at the same moment, and this appearance had prompted her to rescue
disagreement from the vulgar realm of accident. She did what she could
to erect it into a law—a much more edifying aspect of it—by going to
live in Florence, where she bought a house and established herself; and
by leaving her husband to take care of the English branch of his bank.
This arrangement greatly pleased her; it was so felicitously definite. It
struck her husband in the same light, in a foggy square in London, where
it was at times the most definite fact he discerned; but he would have
preferred that such unnatural things should have a greater vagueness.
To agree to disagree had cost him an effort; he was ready to agree to
almost anything but that, and saw no reason why either assent or dissent
should be so terribly consistent.

Mrs Touchett indulged in no regrets nor speculations, and usually
came once a year to spend a month with her husband, a period during
which she apparently took pains to convince him that she had adopted
the right system. She was not fond of the English style of life, and had
three or four reasons for it to which she currently alluded; they bore
upon minor points of that ancient order, but for Mrs Touchett they
amply justified non-residence. She detested bread-sauce, which, as she
said, looked like a poultice and tasted like soap; she objected to the
consumption of beer by her maid-servants; and she affirmed that the
British laundress (Mrs Touchett was very particular about the appearance
of her linen) was not a mistress of her art.[2]

Here the description depends for its effect entirely on the quality
of the author's wit, his organised intellectual comment, and the
wit is of the sort (a penetrating delicacy of observation within an
accepted social group) achieved by Jane Austen or George Eliot.

But some of the described characters in *The Portrait of a Lady*
come poetically to life. This is the description of Isabel's first meeting with the Countess Gemini.

The Countess Gemini simply nodded without getting up; Isabel could
see she was a woman of high fashion. She was thin and dark and not at
all pretty, having features that suggested some tropical bird—a long

beak-like nose, small, quickly-moving eyes and a mouth and chin that receded extremely. Her expression, however, thanks to various intensities of emphasis and wonder, of horror and joy, was not inhuman, and, as regards her appearance, it was plain she understood herself and made the most of her points. Her attire, voluminous and delicate, bristling with elegance, had the look of shimmering plumage, and her attitudes were as light and sudden as those of a creature who perched upon twigs. She had a great deal of manner; Isabel, who had never known anyone with so much manner, immediately classed her as the most affected of women. She remembered that Ralph had not recommended her as an acquaintance; but she was ready to acknowledge that to a casual view the Countess Gemini revealed no depths. Her demonstrations suggested the violent wavings of some flag of general truce—white silk with fluttering streamers.[3]

We are never to get to know the Countess very well, but already we see her with a peculiar vividness, the vividness evoked by poetic imagery. The bird image has a visual force so intense that it goes beyond surface illumination—'bristling with elegance' in its context contains a world of comment as well as vividness. So does the image of the flag of truce.

Henry James's predominant interest is, however, by no means in character. *The Portrait of a Lady*, he tells us in his Preface, has as its corner-stone 'the conception of a certain young woman affronting her destiny'. The interest, it is already indicated, is not primarily a psychological one, not a matter of mere personal analysis. And *The Portrait of a Lady* is indeed a novel of the widest scope and relevance. Though it is in the line of Jane Austen it has a quality which it is not misleading to call symbolic (already we have hinted at a link with what would appear at first to be a wholly different novel, *Wuthering Heights*). *The Portrait of a Lady* is a novel about destiny. Or, to use a concept rather more in tone with the language of the book itself, it is a novel about freedom. It would not be outrageous, though it might be misleading, to call it a nineteenth-century *Paradise Lost*.

Henry James is, of course, far too sophisticated an artist to offer us the 'subject' of his book on a platter. In his moral interest he avoids like the plague anything approaching the abstract.

I might envy [he writes in his Preface], though I couldn't emulate, the imaginative writer so constituted as to see his fable first and to make out its agents afterwards: I could think so little of any fable that didn't need its agents positively to launch it; I could think so little of any situation that didn't depend for its interest on the nature of the persons situated, and thereby on their way of taking it.

And again, a little later:

There is, I think, no more nutritive or suggestive truth in this con-
nexion than that of the perfect dependence of the 'moral' sense of a work
of art on the amount of felt life concerned in producing it.*

James's novel is not a moral fable; but its moral interest is nevertheless central. Only the business of 'launching', of presenting with
all the necessary depth of 'felt life', that 'ado' which is the story of
Isabel Archer, all this may easily distract our attention from the
central theme. Indeed there was a time when James's novels apparently were regarded as 'comedies of manners' (cf. Trollope) and
even so superbly intelligent a reader as E. M. Forster seems to have
missed the point of them almost completely.

The launching of *The Portrait of a Lady* is beautifully done.
Gardencourt, the house in Albany, upper-class London: they are
called up with magnificent certainty and solidity. So too are the
people of the book: the Touchetts, Caspar Goodwood, Henrietta
Stackpole, Lord Warburton, Isabel herself. If these characters are
to contribute to a central pattern it will not be, it is clear, in the
manner of anything approaching allegory. They are all too 'round',
too 'free', to be felt, for even a moment, simply to be 'standing for'
anything. It is one of Henry James's achievements that he can
convince us that his characters have a life outside the pages of his
novel without ever leading us into the temptation of following
them beyond his purpose. It is because everything in these early
chapters of *The Portrait of a Lady* is realised with such fullness,
such apparent lack of pointed emphasis, that we are slow to recognise the basic pattern of the novel, but it is also on this account that
our imagination is so firmly engaged.

Before the end of the first chapter, however, a subsidiary theme
has already been fairly fully stated and three of the main themes
announced or, at any rate, indicated. The subsidiary theme is that
generally referred to in Henry James's novels as the international
situation—the relation of America to Europe. Graham Greene in
a recent introduction to *The Portrait of a Lady* has tried to play
down the importance of this theme. 'It is true the innocent figure is
nearly always American (Roderick Hudson, Newman, Isabel and

---

* I quote with some uneasiness from James's Preface (written, it will be recalled,
some quarter of a century after the novel), not because I doubt the relevance or
interest of his observations but because I am conscious of the difficulty of assimilating
out of context sentences written in his most idiosyncratic, complex style.

Milly, Maggie Verver and her father), but the corrupted characters
. . . are also American: Mme Merle, Gilbert Osmond, Kate Croy,
Merton Densher, Charlotte Stant. His characters are mainly
American, simply because James himself was American.'[4] In fact,
of course, neither Kate Croy nor Densher is an American and one
of the points about the other 'corrupted' characters is that they
are all expatriates, europeanised Americans, whom it is at least
possible to see as corrupted by Europe.* The theme of the impact
of European civilisation on Americans—innocent or not—is not
a main theme of *The Portrait of a Lady* but it is nevertheless there
and we shall return to it later. And it is broached in the
very first pages of the novel in the description of the Touchett
ménage and in such details as the failure of Mr Touchett to understand (or rather, his pretence at not understanding) Lord Warburton's jokes

The main themes indicated in the first chapters are the importance of wealth, the difficulty of marriage and—fundamental to the
other two—the problem of freedom or independence. In each case
the theme appears to be merely a casual subject of conversation but
in fact there is nothing casual there. The vital theme of freedom is
introduced in the form of a joke—one of Mrs Touchett's eccentric
telegrams: ' "Changed hotel, very bad, impudent clerk, address
here. Taken sister's girl, died last year, go to Europe, two sisters,
quite independent".' The telegram is discussed by Mr Touchett
and Ralph.

'There's one thing very clear in it,' said the old man; 'she has given
the hotel-clerk a dressing.'
'I'm not sure even of that, since he has driven her from the field. We
thought at first that the sister mentioned might be the sister of the
clerk; but the subsequent mention of a niece seems to prove that the
allusion is to one of my aunts. Then there was a question as to whose the
two other sisters were; they are probably two of my late aunt's daughters.
But who's "quite independent", and in what sense is the term used?—
that point's not yet settled. Does the expression apply more particularly
to the young lady my mother has adopted, or does it characterise her
sisters equally?—and is it used in a moral or in a financial sense? Does it
mean that they've been left well off, or that they wish to be under no
obligations?—or does it simply mean that they're fond of their own
way?'[5]

---

* For a fuller discussion of this problem see *Henry James, the Major Phase* by
F. O. Matthiessen and *Maule's Curse* by Yvor Winters.

Ralph's frivolous speculations do in fact state the basic problems to be dealt with in the novel. The point is indeed not yet settled: it will take the whole book to settle it. And, even then, 'settle' is not the right word. One does not, Henry James would be quick to remind us, settle life.

The independence of Isabel is the quality about her most often emphasised. Mrs Touchett has taken her up, but she is not, she assures Ralph 'a candidate for adoption'. ' "I'm very fond of my liberty",'[6] she adds. From the very first the ambiguous quality of this independence is stressed. Isabel is attractive, interesting, 'fine' ('she carried within her a great fund of life, and her deepest enjoyment was to feel the continuity between the movements of her own soul and the agitations of the world'[7]); but she is also in many respects inexperienced, naïve. ' "It occurred to me," Mrs Touchett says, "that it would be a kindness to take her about and introduce her to the world. She thinks she knows a great deal of it—like most American girls; but like most American girls she's ridiculously mistaken".'[8] Henry James does not allow us, charming creature as she is, to idealise Isabel:

Altogether, with her meagre knowledge, her inflated ideals, her confidence at once innocent and dogmatic, her temper at once exacting and indulgent, her mixture of curiosity and fastidiousness, of vivacity and indifference, her desire to look very well and to be if possible even better, her determination to see, to try, to know, her combination of the delicate desultory flame-like spirit and the eager and personal creature of conditions: she would be an easy victim of scientific criticism: if she were not intended to awaken on the reader's part an impulse more tender and more purely expectant.[9]

The Portrait of a Lady is the revelation of the inadequacy of Isabel's view to freedom.

The revelation is so full, so concrete, that to abstract from it the main, insistent theme must inevitably weaken the impression of the book. But analysis involves such abstraction and we shall not respond fully to James's novel unless we are conscious of its theme. The theme in its earlier stages is fully expressed in the scene in which Caspar Goodwood for the second time asks Isabel to marry him (she has just refused Lord Warburton).

'I don't know,' she answered rather grandly. 'The world—with all these places so arranged and so touching each other—comes to strike one as rather small.'

'It's a sight too big for me!' Caspar exclaimed with a simplicity our young lady might have found touching if her face had not been set against concessions.

This attitude was part of a system, a theory, that she had lately embraced, and to be thorough she said after a moment: 'Don't think me unkind if I say it's just that—being out of your sight—that I like. If you were in the same place I should feel you were watching me, and I don't like that—I like my liberty too much. If there's a thing in the world I'm fond of,' she went on with a slight recurrence of grandeur, 'it's my personal independence.' But whatever there might be of the too superior in this speech moved Caspar Goodwood's admiration; there was nothing he winced at in the large air of it. He had never supposed she hadn't wings and the need of beautiful free movements—he wasn't, with his own long arms and strides, afraid of any force in her. Isabel's words, if they had been meant to shock him, failed of the mark and only made him smile with the sense that here was common ground. 'Who would wish less to curtail your liberty than I? What can give me greater pleasure than to see you perfectly independent—doing whatever you like? It's to make you independent that I want to marry you.'

'That's a beautiful sophism,' said the girl with a smile more beautiful still.

'An unmarried woman—a girl of your age—isn't independent. There are all sorts of things she can't do. She's hampered at every step.'

'That's as she looks at the question,' Isabel answered with much spirit. 'I'm not in my first youth—I can do what I choose—I belong quite to the independent class. I've neither father nor mother; I'm poor and of a serious disposition; I'm not pretty. I therefore am not bound to be timid and conventional; indeed I can't afford such luxuries. Besides, I try to judge things for myself; to judge wrong, I think, is more honourable than not to judge at all. I don't wish to be a mere sheep in the flock; I wish to choose my fate and know something of human affairs beyond what other people think it compatible with propriety to tell me.' She paused a moment, but not long enough for her companion to reply. He was apparently on the point of doing so when she went on: 'Let me say this to you, Mr Goodwood. You're so kind as to speak of being afraid of my marrying. If you should hear a rumour that I'm on the point of doing so —girls are liable to have such things said about them—remember what I have told you about my love of liberty and venture to doubt it.'[10]

The Portrait of a Lady is far from allegory yet one is permitted to feel, in the symbolic quality of the novel, that the characters, though unmistakably individuals, are more than individuals. Thus, in her rejection of Caspar Goodwood, Isabel is rejecting America, or at least that part of America that Goodwood represents, young, strong, go-ahead, uninhibited, hard. For Goodwood (as for

Henrietta, who essentially shares his quality) the problem of freedom is simple and might be expressed in the words of Mr Archibald
Macleish's American Dream:

> America is promises
> For those that take them.

Goodwood—and it would be wrong to see him as a wholly unsympathetic character—is prepared to take them with all that
taking implies. To him and Henrietta (and they are, on one level,
the most sensible, positive people in the book) Isabel's problem is
not a problem at all. Freedom for them has the simple quality it
possessed for the nineteenth-century liberal.

The rejection of Lord Warburton has, similarly, a symbolic
quality—though, again, one must insist that this is not an allegory.
Warburton is a liberal aristocrat. He embodies the aristocratic
culture of Europe (that has so attracted Isabel at Gardencourt) and
adds his own reforming ideas—a combination which Henry James,
had he been the kind of aesthetic snob he is often held to be,
might have found irresistible. Ralph Touchett sums up Warburton's social position magnificently:

'. . . He says I don't understand my time, I understand it certainly
better than he, who can neither abolish himself as a nuisance nor maintain
himself as an institution.'[11]

Isabel's rejection of Lord Warburton is not a light one. She feels
very deeply the attraction of the aristocratic standards. But she feels
also the limitations of Warburton and his sisters, the Misses
Molyneux (it is worth comparing them with another 'county'
family—the Marchants—in the wonderful *Princess Casamassima*;
Henry James's attitude to the British aristocracy is by no means
uncritical).

'. . . So long as I look at the Misses Molyneux they seem to me to
answer a kind of ideal. Then Henrietta presents herself, and I'm straight-
way convinced by *her*; not so much in respect to herself as in respect to
what masses behind her.'[12]

Ralph, too, (though he does not undervalue her) disposes of
Henrietta:

'Henrietta . . . does smell of the Future—it almost knocks one down!'[13]

Goodwood and Warburton rejected (almost like two temptations), Isabel is now 'free' to affront her destiny. But she is not free because she is poor. She has never, we are told early on, known anything about money, and it is typical of this novel that this fine, romantic indifference to wealth should be one of the basic factors in Isabel's tragedy.

Henry James's characters always have to be rich and the reason is not the obvious one. 'I call people rich,' says Ralph Touchett, 'when they're able to meet the requirements of their imagination.'[14] It is for this reason that he persuades his father to leave Isabel a fortune. She must be rich in order to be free of the material world. She must be free in order to 'live'.

It is Ralph's one supreme mistake in intelligence and it is the mistake that ruins Isabel. For it is her wealth that arouses Madame Merle's realisation that she can use her and leads directly to the disastrous, tragic marriage with Osmond. And in the superb scene in which, sitting in the candlelight in the elegant, spiritually empty house in Rome, Isabel takes stock of her tragedy, she painfully reveals to herself the conclusion:

But for her money, as she saw today, she would never have done it. And then her mind wandered off to poor Mr Touchett, sleeping under English turf, the beneficient author of infinite woe! For this was the fantastic fact. At bottom her money had been a burden, had been on her mind, which was filled with the desire to transfer the weight of it to some other conscience, to some more prepared receptacle. What would lighten her own conscience more effectually than to make it over to the man with the best taste in the world? Unless she should have given it to a hospital there would have been nothing better she could do with it; and there was no charitable institution in which she had been as much interested as in Gilbert Osmond. He would use her fortune in a way that would make her think better of it and rub off a certain grossness attaching to the good luck of an unexpected inheritance. There had been nothing very delicate in inheriting seventy thousand pounds; the delicacy had been all in Mr Touchett's leaving them to her. But to marry Gilbert Osmond and bring him such a portion—in that there would be delicacy for her as well. There would be less for him—that was true; but that was his affair, and if he loved her he wouldn't object to her being rich. Had he not had the courage to say he was glad she was rich?[15]

It is at the moment when Ralph is dying that the theme is finally stated in the form at once the most affecting and most morally profound.

She raised her head and her clasped hands; she seemed for a moment to pray for him. 'Is it true—is it true?' she asked.

'True that you've been stupid? Oh no,' said Ralph with a sensible intention of wit.

'That you made me rich—that all I have is yours?'

He turned away his head, and for some time said nothing. Then, at last: 'Ah, don't speak of that—that was not happy.' Slowly he moved his face toward her again, and they once more saw each other.

'But for that—but for that——!' And he paused. 'I believe I ruined you,' he wailed.

She was full of the sense that he was beyond the reach of pain; he seemed already so little of this world. But even if she had not had it she would still have spoken, for nothing mattered now but the only knowledge that was not pure anguish—the knowledge that they were looking at the truth together. 'He married me for the money,' she said. She wished to say everything; she was afraid he might die before she had done so.

He gazed at her a little, and for the first time his fixed eyes lowered their lids. But he raised them in a moment, and then, 'He was greatly in love with you,' he answered.

'Yes, he was in love with me. But he wouldn't have married me if I had been poor. I don't hurt you in saying that. How can I? I only want you to understand. I always tried to keep you from understanding; but that's all over.'

'I always understood,' said Ralph.

'I thought you did, and I didn't like it. But now I like it.'

'You don't hurt me—you make me very happy.' And as Ralph said this there was an extraordinary gladness in his voice. She bent her head again, and pressed her lips to the back of his hand. 'I always understood,' he continued, 'though it was so strange—so pitiful. You wanted to look at life for yourself—but you were not allowed; you were punished for your wish. You were ground in the very mill of the conventional!'

'Oh yes, I've been punished,' Isabel sobbed.[16]

The necessity here of stating in its dreadful simplicity the agonising truth so that the relationship of the two may be purified and deepened shows an intuition the very opposite of sentimental.

Isabel, then, imagining herself free, has in fact delivered herself into bondage. And the bondage has come about not casually but out of the very force and fortune of her own aspirations to freedom. She has sought life and because she has sought it in this way she has found death.

Freedom, to Isabel and to Ralph (for he has been as much concerned in the issue as she), has been an idealised freedom. They have sought to be free not through a recognition of, but by an escape from, necessity. And in so doing they have delivered Isabel over to an exploitation as crude and more corrupting than the exploitation that would have been her fate if Mrs Touchett had never visited Albany.

' "Do you still like Serena Merle?" ' is Mrs Touchett's last question of Isabel.

'Not as I once did. But it doesn't matter, for she's going to America.'
'To America? She must have done something very bad.'
'Yes—very bad.'
'May I ask what it is?'
'She made a convenience of me.'
'Ah,' cried Mrs Touchett, 'so she did of me! She does of everyone.'[17]

The Portrait of a Lady is one of the most profound expressions in literature of the illusion that freedom is an abstract quality inherent in the individual soul.

It is interesting to compare James's book with another great novel written not very long before, *Madame Bovary*, the story of another woman 'ground in the very mill of the conventional'. It is true that Emma Bovary is, unlike Isabel Archer, not in the least 'fine', that she fails to escape from her petty-bourgeois social *milieu* and that she is quite incapable of the exalted moral discipline to which Isabel is dedicated, yet we will learn something of James's novel, I think, from a glance at Flaubert's. What is shocking in *Madame Bovary* is the appalling passivity of Flaubert's characters, their inability to fight in any effective way the bourgeois world which Flaubert detests and which relentlessly warps and destroys all fineness in them. The strength of the novel lies in the very ruthlessness of its exposure of romantic attitudes; but therein also lies its weakness, the sense we get of something less than the human capacity for heroism, the uneasy suspicions of a *roman à thèse*. *The Portrait of a Lady* gives, as a matter of fact, no more positive response to its revelation of bourgeois values than *Madame Bovary*, yet we do experience a sense of human resilience and dignity. The interesting question is how far this sense—embodied in the 'fineness' of Isabel herself—is merely romantic and illusory.

The issue can perhaps be put in this way: is not the accumulated effect of the novel to present human destiny as inexorably one of suffering and despair? There are a number of tendencies making for this effect. In the first place there is the insistent use of dramatic irony in the construction of the book. Chapter after chapter in the

early reaches of the novel is designed to emphasise the fatality
facing Isabel's aspirations. The fifth chapter tells us she has come
to Europe to find happiness; the sixth that she likes unexpectedness
('I shall not have success [in Europe] if they're too stupidly conventional. I'm not in the least stupidly conventional'). The seventh
chapter ends with the following exchange:

> 'I always want to know the things one shouldn't do.'
> 'So as to do them?' asked her aunt.
> 'So as to choose,' said Isabel.

The eighth draws to a close with

> 'I shall never make anyone a martyr.'
> 'You'll never be one, I hope.'
> 'I hope not. . . .'

This is all, it may be argued, simply Henry James at work, extract-
ing from every situation its maximum of point. But the art, it seems
to me, is in a subtle sense self-betraying. What is achieved is a
kind of inevitability, a sense of Isabel's never standing a chance,
which amounts not to objective irony but to the creation of something like an external destiny. Is not martyrdom becoming, in a
sense at once insidious and—with all the associations and overtones
one may care to give the word—romantic? Is there not to be here a
breath—a very sophisticated and infinitely worldly breath—of the
emotional and moral inadequacy involved in George Eliot's vision
of those latter-day Saint Theresas?

Our final judgement must depend on the climax—the famous
ending—of the book. It is from this ultimate impression that we
shall have to decide whether James indeed plays fair with Isabel
and us, whether he reveals in full profundity and (in the least cold
sense of the word) objectivity a tragic situation or whether there is
a certain sleight of hand, the putting across not of life but of something which merely for the moment passes for life. But before we
consider this final climax it is worth noting what would seem an
odd weakness in the novel. Is it not a little strange that of all the
essential parts of Isabel's story which are revealed to us the section
of her life most pointedly avoided is that immediately before her
decision to marry Osmond? She has met him, got to know him
somewhat; she then goes away for a year, travelling in Europe and
the Middle East with Madame Merle. When she comes back to

Florence she has decided to marry Osmond. This is, from the novelist's point of view, the most difficult moment in the book. How to convince us that a young woman like Isabel would in fact marry a man like Osmond? And it is a moment which, despite the revealing conversation with Ralph (which does indeed tell us something) is, I suggest, not satisfactorily got over. And the point is that if Isabel's marriage to Osmond is in any sense a fraud perpetrated upon us for his own ends by the author, the book is greatly weakened.

At the end of the novel Isabel, after Ralph's death and another encounter with Caspar Goodwood, returns to Rome. Is her return to Osmond irrevocable, an acceptance now and for ever of her 'destiny', or is it tentative, no ending, the situation unresolved? Mr F. O. Matthiessen, arguing in the latter sense, has a most interesting observation:

> The end of Isabel's career is not yet in sight. That fact raises a critical issue about James's way of rounding off his narratives. He was keenly aware of what his method involved. As he wrote in his notebook, upon concluding his detailed project: 'With strong handling it seems to me that it may be all very true, very powerful, very touching. The obvious criticism of course will be that it is not finished—that it has not seen the heroine to the end of her situation—that I have left her *en l'air*. This is both true and false. The *whole* of anything is never told; you can only take what groups together. What I have done has that unity—it groups together. It is complete in itself—and the rest may be taken up or not, later.'[18]

James's own evidence is of course conclusive as to his intention, but it is not necessarily relevant as to what is in fact achieved; and it seems to me that, although the ending of *The Portrait of a Lady* does not completely and irrevocably round off the story—the possibility of Isabel's later reconsidering her decision is not excluded—yet the dominant impression is undoubtedly that of the deliberate rejection of 'life' (as offered by Caspar Goodwood) in favour of death, as represented by the situation in Rome. The scene with Goodwood is indeed very remarkable with its candid, if tortured, facing of a sexual implication which James is apt to sheer off. On the whole the effect of this scene, though one understands completely the quality of Isabel's reaction, is further to weight the scales against a return to Rome. Even if Goodwood himself is impossible, the vitality that he conveys is a force to be reckoned with and Isabel's rejection of this vitality involves more clearly than ever the sense that she is turning her face to the wall.

Isabel's return to Rome is certainly not a mere surrender to the conventional force of the marriage vow. The issue as to whether or not she should leave her husband is twice quite frankly broached by Henrietta, as well as by Goodwood. Isabel's first reply to Henrietta is significant:

> 'I don't know what great unhappiness might bring me to; but it seems to me I shall always be ashamed. One must accept one's deeds. I married him before all the world; I was perfectly free; it was impossible to do anything more deliberate. One can't change that way,' Isabel repeated.[19]

Later, when she discovers how little free she had in fact been, it is her obligation towards Pansy that becomes the most important factor. But always there is the sense of some deep inward consideration that makes the particular issues—the character of Osmond, her own mistakes, the needs of Pansy, the importunity of Goodwood—irrelevant. The recurring image in the last pages is of a sea or torrent in which Isabel is immersed. Goodwood becomes identified with the torrent. Her temptation is to give herself up to it.* When she breaks loose from him and the image she is once more 'free', free and in darkness. The lights now are the lights of Gardencourt and now he knows where to turn. 'There was a very straight path.'[20]

It seems to me inescapable that what Isabel finally chooses is something represented by a high cold word like duty or resignation, the duty of an empty vow, the resignation of the defeated, and that in making her choice she is paying a final sacrificial tribute to her own ruined conception of freedom. For Henry James, though he sees the tragedy implicit in the Victorian ruling-class view of freedom, is himself so deeply involved in that illusion that he cannot escape from it. His books are tragedies precisely because their subject is the smashing of the bourgeois illusion of freedom in the consciousness of characters who are unable to conceive of freedom in any other way. His 'innocent' persons have therefore always the characters of victims; they are at the mercy of the vulgar and the corrupt, and the more finely conscious they become of their situation the more unable are they to cope with it in positive terms. Hence the contradiction of a Fleda Vetch† whose superior conscious-

---

* It is at such a moment that one sees the force of Stephen Spender's linking of James with Conrad's 'in the destructive element immerse' in an otherwise not very helpful book (*The Destructive Element*, 1937).

† In *The Spoils of Poynton*.

ness (and conscience) leads her in effect to reject life in favour of death. This is a favourite, almost an archetypal situation, in James's novels. It achieves its most striking expression in *The Portrait of a Lady* and *The Wings of the Dove* in which another rich American girl meets, even more powerfully and more exquisitely, the fate of Isabel Archer.

For James in his supreme concern for 'living' (Milly Theale in *The Wings of the Dove*, Strether in *The Ambassadors* have, like Isabel, this immense, magnificent desire to 'live') ultimately, in effect, turns his back on life. This is not unconnected, I think, with the fact that his characters never do anything like work. This description of Madame Merle is not untypical of a day in the life of a Henry James figure:

When Madame Merle was neither writing, nor painting, nor touching the piano, she was usually employed upon wonderful tasks of rich embroidery, cushions, curtains, decorations for the chimney-piece; an art in which her bold, free invention was as noted as the agility of her needle. She was never idle, for when engaged in none of the ways I have mentioned she was either reading (she appeared to Isabel to read 'everything important'), or walking out, or playing patience with the cards, or talking with her fellow inmates.[21]

The contemplation of such a way of life is likely, after all, to lead to idealism, for the necessities behind such an existence are by no means obvious. It is a superficial criticism to accuse James of snobbery or even of being limited by his social environment (what artist is not?). But there can be no doubt that what the bourgeois world did for James was to turn him into a moral idealist chasing a chimera of ideal conduct divorced from social reality.

It is not that his sense of social reality is in any way weak. On the contrary his picture of his world has, it has already been emphasised, a magnificent solidity, a concrete richness of the subtlest power. Nor is he in any easy, obvious sense taken in by that world (note his attitude to Warburton, his description of American-French society in chapter XX and his total contempt for Osmond and his values); his picture of European bourgeois life is in its objective aspect as realistic as that of Balzac or Flaubert or Proust. No, if we are to isolate in James's novels the quality that is ultimately their limitation, it is to the core of his point of view, his philosophy, that we are led. The limiting factor in *The Portrait of a Lady* is the failure of James in the last analysis to dissociate himself from Isabel's errors of understanding.

One of the central recurring themes of James's novels is the desire to 'live', to achieve a fullness of consciousness which permits the richest yet most exquisite response to the vibrations of life. And yet with this need to live is associated almost invariably the sense of death. Living, he seems to be saying again and again, involves martyrdom. The pleasure he finds in the contemplation and description of living at its most beautiful, most exalted point is subtly increased if the living creature is faced with death. Ralph Touchett is not alone among the dying swans of James's books: he is one of a line culminating in Strether (who discovers how to live too late) and in the fabulous Milly Theale. The attraction of this subject to James seems to me most significant. 'Very true . . . very powerful . . . very touching . . .' one can almost hear him breathing out the words. It is a kind of apotheosis of his vision of life. And it is intimately, inextricably, linked up with his philosophic idealism. His 'good' characters, in their unswerving effort to live finely, turn out to be in the full implication of the phrase, too good for this world. Their sensibility becomes an end in itself, not a response to the actual issues of life. The freedom they seek turns out to be an idealised freedom; its ends, therefore, can only end, in a desire not merely to be free *in* this world but to be free *of* this world.

The popularity of James's novels among our intelligentsia today is significant too. It includes, I feel certain, not merely a genuine admiration for his extraordinary qualities, but also a powerful element of self-indulgence. It is not only pleasanter but easier to involve oneself in an idealised sensibility, a conscience* removed into realms outside the common and often crude basis of actual living. Many besides Isabel Archer imagine that they can buy themselves out of the crudities through the means of a high-grade consciousness and a few thousand pounds. And Henry James, albeit unconsciously, offers a subtle encouragement. He expresses the fate of Isabel Archer but expresses it in a way that suggests that it has, if not inevitability, at least a kind of glory to it. So that when Isabel takes her decision to return to Rome the dominant sense is not of the waste and degradation of a splendid spirit, but of a kind of inverted triumph. Better death than a surrender of the illusion which the novel has so richly and magnificently and tragically illuminated.

* It is interesting to speculate whether Conrad, when he referred to James as 'the historian of fine consciences', was using the word in its English sense or with the French implication of 'consciousness'.

3

SAMUEL BUTLER: THE *WAY OF ALL FLESH*

(Written 1872–84, published 1903)

'Well,' he continued, 'there are a lot of things that want saying which no one dares to say, a lot of shams which want attacking, and yet no one attacks them. It seems to me that I can say things which not another man in England except myself will venture to say, and yet which are crying to be said.'[1]

It was once the fashion to say of *The Way of All Flesh* that it is not really a novel at all. No one, however, has attempted to suggest what it is if it is not a novel. The truth is that any definition of the novel that excluded Samuel Butler's book would also exclude about a quarter of the novels—at any rate, the good novels—ever written. The truth is also that the opponents of Butler's *ideas*, wishing (whether consciously or not) to discredit those ideas, have appreciated that one effective line of attack is to deny his book the status of art; while his supporters, realising that much of the exhilaration they derive from the book is not—in the narrow sense—an 'aesthetic' one, have tended to take the line that if this isn't art it is something better. I think it is important to insist that *The Way of All Flesh* is art, that it is life-conveying fantasy and not an essay or a sermon or a textbook. It may well be that certain elements in the novel—elements connected with Butler's propagandist intentions —do indeed weaken it as a work of art, but that is another matter. For we shall also find, I believe, that the artistic strength of the book—its power to stimulate our imagination—is also closely connected with Butler's propagandist intentions. As with every good novel the book and the 'message' are inseparable. The point about *The Way of All Flesh* is not that it has more 'message' than, say, *The Portrait of a Lady* but that the 'message' is more obviously contentious and more clearly related to immediate action.

The 'message' of *The Way of All Flesh* is almost purely negative. The novel is a hymn of hate against Victorian Christianity and the Victorian bourgeois family. And when these two institutions are united in what might be regarded as their highest form—a clergyman's family—the challenge is met with a weapon of invective as devastating as Voltaire's.

The clergyman is expected to be a kind of human Sunday. Things must not be done in him which are venial in the week-day classes. He is paid for this business of leading a stricter life than other people. It is his *raison d'être*. If his parishioners feel that he does this, they approve of him, for they look upon him as their own contribution towards what they deem a holy life. This is why the clergyman is so often called a vicar—he being the person whose vicarious goodness is to stand for that of those entrusted to his charge. But home is his castle as much as that of any other Englishman, and with him, as with others, unnatural tension in public is followed by exhaustion when tension is no longer necessary. His children are the most defenceless things he can reach, and it is on them in nine cases out of ten that he will relieve his mind.[2]

Clearly a novelist who permits himself—in his role of commentator—such asides is weighting the scales against himself as an artist. For unless the fantastic world he succeeds in creating is extraordinarily solid, extraordinarily convincing to the reader, one will be bound to have the sense of being 'got at'. There is no reason whatever why such asides should not be made in a novel (we recall Fielding, Stendhal, Tolstoy, George Eliot), but to be accepted by the reader, they must always be appreciable within the total experience of the novel as a work of art. When George Eliot, in *Middlemarch*, pauses to discuss the failure of the Lydgates' marriage we are in no way offended by her intrusion because the issues concerned have been so fully and concretely presented to our imagination that such discussion seems natural and necessary within the imaginative framework of the book. In *The Way of All Flesh* the problem is more perilous. We are so constantly aware of Butler's *views* (the narrator, Overton, is never seriously 'placed', never separated from Butler himself) which are presented with such verve and passionate wit, that there is a serious danger that the vitality of the comment may overtop the vitality of the world of the novel.

I do not think that this does in fact happen, at any rate in the earlier parts of the book. In the sections dealing with the older generations of Pontifexes and with Ernest's childhood Butler's invective does have an 'objective correlative'. The invective is shattering—'Yet when a man is very fond of his money it is not easy for him at all times to be very fond of his children also',[3]—'I think the Church Catechism has a good deal to do with the unhappy relations which commonly even now exist between parents and children'[4]—but it is a real world that is shattered, not a set of ninepins. Scene after scene in this part of the book is superbly successful. Old Mrs John Pontifex refusing to take cognizance of her pregnancy; the hilarious episode in which George Pontifex and his butler go down to the cellar to fetch the bottle of water from the Jordan; the incident of the hen lobster; the scene in the carriage after Theobald's marriage to Christina; the chastisement of the infant Ernest for his inability to say 'come': these are scenes not merely effective as anecdotes (all Butler's episodes have this quality) but magnificently alive and solid. A world as convincing as—in their different ways—the workhouse world of *Oliver Twist* or the world of Gardencourt is here evoked.

This is the description of the dinner on the eve of Ernest's christening:

Her father [George Pontifex], of course, was the lion of the party, but seeing that we were all meek and quite willing to be eaten, he roared to us rather than at us. It was a fine sight to see him tucking his napkin under his rosy old gills, and letting it fall over his capacious waistcoat while the high light from the chandelier danced about the bump of benevolence on his bald old head like a star of Bethlehem.

The soup was real turtle; the old gentleman was evidently well pleased and he was beginning to come out. Gelstrap stood behind his master's chair. I sat next Mrs Theobald on her left hand, and was thus just opposite her father-in-law, whom I had every opportunity of observing.

During the first ten minutes or so, which were taken up with the soup and the bringing in of the fish, I should probably have thought if I had not long since made up my mind about him, what a fine old man he was and how proud his children should be of him; but suddenly as he was helping himself to lobster sauce, he flushed crimson, a look of extreme vexation suffused his face, and he darted two furtive but fiery glances to the two ends of the table, one for Theobald and one for Christina. They, poor simple souls, of course saw that something was exceedingly wrong, and so did I, but I couldn't guess what it was till I heard the old man hiss in Christina's ear:

'It was not made with a hen lobster. What's the use,' he continued, 'of my calling the boy Ernest, and getting him christened in water from the Jordan, if his own father does not know a cock from a hen lobster?'[5]

It is worth noticing in this magnificent scene one phrase at the

beginning of the third paragraph—'. . . I should probably have
thought, if I had not long since made up my mind about him. . . .'
It is a tell-tale phrase, weakening as it does the dramatic development of the episode. Overton/Butler is dissociating himself from
the scene. He always does. He cannot allow us to imagine, even for
a moment, that he does not know better than the Pontifexes. In this
particular scene it does not matter much. But the cumulative effect
is dangerous. For it tends to give the book a somewhat abstract
quality, to put the characters at a distance which precludes the
reader's intimate involvement and this increases the tendency for
the vitality of the narrator's comment to overtop the vitality of the
fantastic world.

The Way of All Flesh is not, in the sense I have previously used
the term, a moral fable. But the seed from which it springs is con-
tained in the sentence quoted at the head of this chapter. The words
are in the mouth of Ernest Pontifex but they are Butler's own. To
attack shams, to reveal horrors, to strike (no punches pulled) at
the darling sanctities of the Victorian bourgeoisie: this is the
motive-force behind the novel. It is a propagandist novel, which
means that the author is quite consciously concerned not merely
to interpret facts but to change them.

There is today a good deal of prejudice against the idea of propaganda. We tend to suspect the 'novel with a purpose', forgetting
perhaps that the important thing about a book is not its purpose
but its effect. (Its purpose is relevant only in so far as we are
concerned to analyse the causes of the achieved effect.) Now every
novel, for better or for worse, achieves some effect and it is an
effect made not in a vacuum but upon us. Every novel we read must,
to some extent (be it ever so little or ever so temporarily), change
us. According to the degree of effect which it achieves it will (nearly
always without our realising it) influence our actions. Every novel is
in this sense propagandist and it is as well to bear that fact in mind.

What we can legitimately object to in a novel is not that it should
change us but that it should unsuccessfully attempt to do so. What
we really mean as a rule when we criticise a novel as 'propagandist'
is that the total imaginative effect of the book is unconvincing and the
author has therefore failed in his purpose of achieving a certain effect.

The Way of All Flesh, brilliant and stimulating book as it is,
fails to be a great novel not because it is consciously propagandist
but because certain aspects of Butler's propaganda are not good
enough. On its negative side—the attack on shams—it is, broadly
speaking, superb; the weakness lies in its positive side. There fails

to emerge from the novel—except at the moments when what is loathsome is being demolished—a sense of the vitality of life itself. That this criticism is, however, less crippling than it might be is appreciated when we recall that for more than two-thirds of the book negative themes prevail. Up to the imprisonment of Ernest, Butler is for the bulk of the time securely attached to his hatreds, an attachment symbolised by the perverse insistence of Overton in maintaining a friendship with Theobald whom he detests.

It would be an exaggeration to insist that the first two-thirds of the novel is wholly successful. Our most serious doubt lies in the presentation of Theobald himself. Does Butler ever give him a chance? The doubt arises, I think, less from any inherent improbability in the character (there must have been parsons who out-Theobalded Theobald) than from touches of over-eagerness on Butler's part. There he is, we feel, pen in hand, for ever poised to pounce, and the spectacle is not only a little undignified (we are quite ready to sacrifice dignity on the bonfire of bourgeois pomposity) but rather repellent, like the journalist who follows the Cabinet minister around waiting for the chance indiscretion. There is an unholy glee behind the unmasking of Theobald which gives the impression, perhaps, that some of the operation is being performed for the satisfaction of Butler rather than ourselves and it is this suspicion, or something like it, that weakens the effect.

I do not wish to suggest that *The Way of All Flesh* would have been a better book if Butler had been, in the conventional sense, more 'fair-minded' and less partisan. On the contrary, it is precisely his partisanship, his bold and righteous indignation against the cant of conventional bourgeois life that gives his novel its unique and exhilarating flavour. It is worth recalling that scene in *Wuthering Heights* in which Cathy and Heathcliff throw their pious books into the dog-kennel and comparing it with the following description of a Sunday evening from *The Way of All Flesh*:

In the course of the evening they [the children] came into the drawing-room, and, as an especial treat, were to sing some of their hymns to me, instead of saying them, so that I might hear how nicely they sang. Ernest was to choose the first hymn, and he chose one about some people who were to come to the sunset tree. I am no botanist, and do not know what kind of tree a sunset tree is, but the words began, 'Come, come, come; come to the sunset tree for the day is past and gone'.

The tune was rather pretty and had taken Ernest's fancy, for he was unusually fond of music and had a sweet little child's voice which he liked using.

He was, however, very late in being able to sound a hard 'c' or 'k', and, instead of saying 'Come', he said 'Tum, tum, tum'.

'Ernest,' said Theobald, from the arm-chair in front of the fire, where he was sitting with his hands folded before him, 'don't you think it would be very nice if you were to say "come" like other people instead of "tum"?'

'I do say "tum",' replied Ernest, meaning that he had said 'come'.

Theobald was always in a bad temper on Sunday evening. Whether it is that they are as much bored with the day as their neighbours, or whether they are tired, or whatever the cause may be, clergymen are seldom at their best on Sunday evening; I had already seen signs that evening that my host was cross, and was a little nervous at hearing Ernest say so promptly, 'I do say "tum",' when his papa had said he did not say it as he should.

Theobald noticed the fact that he was being contradicted in a moment. He got up from his arm-chair and went to the piano.

'No, Ernest, you don't,' he said, 'you say nothing of the kind, you say "tum", not "come". Now say "come" after me, as I do.'

'Tum,' said Ernest, at once; 'is that better?' I have no doubt he thought it was, but it was not.

'Now, Ernest, you are not taking pains; you are not trying as you ought to do. It is high time you learned to say "come", why, Joey can say "come", can't you, Joey?'

'Yeth, I can,' replied Joey, and he said something which was not far off 'come'.

'There, Ernest, do you hear that? There's no difficulty about it, nor shadow of difficulty. Now, take your own time, think about it, and say "come" after me.'

The boy remained silent a few seconds and then said 'tum' again.

I laughed, but Theobald turned to me impatiently and said, 'Please do not laugh, Overton; it will make the boy think it does not matter, and it matters a great deal;' then turning to Ernest he said, 'Now, Ernest, I will give you one more chance, and if you don't say "come", I shall know that you are self-willed and naughty.'

He looked very angry, and a shade came over Ernest's face, like that which comes upon the face of a puppy when it is being scolded without understanding why. The child saw well what was coming now, was frightened, and, of course, said 'tum' once more.

'Very well, Ernest,' said his father, catching him angrily by the shoulder. 'I have done my best to save you, but if you will have it so, you will,' and he lugged the little wretch, crying by anticipation, out of the room. A few minutes more and we could hear screams coming from the dining-room, across the hall which separated the drawing-room from the dining-room, and knew that poor Ernest was being beaten.

'I have sent him up to bed,' said Theobald, as he returned to the drawing-room, 'and now, Christina, I think we will have the servants in to prayers,' and he rang the bell for them, red-handed as he was.[6]

This seems to me entirely successful, the indignation controlled and organised to supreme effect. The remark of Theobald's to Ernest (aged four): 'There's no difficulty about it, nor shadow of difficulty . . .' not only comments perfectly on the quality of Theobald's understanding of his son but tells us all we need to know about his rhetorical style in the pulpit. The use of the younger child as a stick to prod the elder recalls an earlier remark in the book:

> The boys were of use to their father in one respect. I mean that he played them off against each other.[7]

an example of Butler's wit at its most economical. And the adjective 'red-handed' in the last sentence is masterly, bearing precisely the right proportions of horror and of laughter.

But against the triumphant presentation of such a scene as this, one must note a number which are less than convincing. Nothing about Alethea Pontifex quite comes to life, nor do the theological arguments in Cambridge or London really force their way into the book. And by now we are beginning to feel the true weakness of the novel—the lack of any positive values which can balance emotionally the gusto with which the negative points are made. The ultimate weakness of *The Way of All Flesh* has been indicated by Mr V. S. Pritchett:

> One ends with the feeling that Ernest Pontifex doesn't amount to much. . . . One does not feel that Ernest has very deeply developed because of suffering or fortune. He has escaped only. And he seems rather lost without his enemy. The weakness is that Butler is doing all the talking. There is no contradictory principle. Ultimately, the defence of orthodoxy, even an orthodoxy as dim as Theobald's, is the knowledge of human passions. The strange thing is that Ernest does not give us the impression of a man who enjoys himself; he sounds like a man whose hedonism is a prig's hygiene. He looks like becoming the average bachelor of the room marked Residents Only.[8]

This seems to me on the whole a fair comment on the last part of *The Way of All Flesh*. Ernest has come through; but what has he come to? A comfortable fortune, a conveniently bigamous marriage, and the company of a number of elderly gentlemen who appreciate his views on theology. Because he is rich he is able to dispense with family life, farming out his children on those unfortunately unable to afford the same luxury. *There is no contradictory principle.* And the truth is, of course, that Butler himself, vigorous and ruthless as is his analysis of certain facets of the society he lived in, is in the end a Victorian bourgeois himself, an eccentric, not a revolutionary.

And yet that is not the whole truth either. There are insights in *The Way of All Flesh* far more profound than the term 'eccentric' could suggest. It is true that Alethea Pontifex's legacy and those cosy chambers in the Temple with geraniums in the window weaken the force of Ernest's rebellion against his respectable family. It is true that Ernest is not much more of a hero than Oliver Twist and that his comparative passivity (he is in the line of Heart-free rather than Tom Jones) is one of the reasons for the weakness of the positive elements of the book. And it is true, too, that when he has got his freedom Ernest does mighty little with it. All this is undeniable; yet the fact remains that *The Way of All Flesh* tells more of the truth about the Victorian age than any other novel of the century excepting Dickens's books and *Wuthering Heights*.

Its secret can, I believe, be suggested by an examination of two episodes. The first takes place when Ernest—twenty-three years old and ordained Deacon—is living in Ashpit Place, having 'gone amongst the poor' (inspired, significantly enough, by *Alton Locke*, Dickens's novels and other 'literary garbage'). Ernest is at this time in the clutches alternately of Evangelists and High Churchmen—all humbugs—and one day he meets his old Cambridge friend Towneley, the young man-about-town-cum-rowing-blue (a character in whom, incidentally, some of the oddities of Butler's positives emerge).

Towneley said a few words of common form to Ernest about his profession as being what he thought would be most likely to interest him, and Ernest, still confused and shy, gave him for lack of something better to say his little threepenny-bit about poor people being so very nice. Towneley took this for what it was worth and nodded assent, whereon Ernest imprudently went further and said, 'Don't you like poor people very much yourself?'

Towneley gave his face a comical but good-natured screw, and said quietly, but slowly and decidedly, 'No, no, no,' and escaped.

It was all over with Ernest from that moment. As usual he did not know it, but he had entered none the less upon another reaction. Towneley had just taken Ernest's threepenny-bit into his hands, looked at it and returned it to him as a bad one. Why did he see in a moment that it was a bad one now, though he had been unable to see it when he had taken it from Pryer? Of course some poor people were very nice, and always would be so, but as though scales had fallen suddenly from his eyes he saw that no one was nicer for being poor, and that between the upper and lower classes there was a gulf which amounted practically to an impassable barrier.

That evening he reflected a good deal. If Towneley was right, and Ernest felt that the 'No' had applied not to the remark about poor people only, but to the whole scheme and scope of his recently adopted ideas, he and Pryer must surely be on a wrong tack. Towneley had not argued with him; he had said one word only, and that one of the shortest in the language, but Ernest was in a fit state for inoculation, and the minute particle of virus set about working immediately.[9]

One might quote the passage as an example of Butler's Disraelian realism (it is worth comparing *The Way of All Flesh* with *Sybil* or *Coningsby*), but what seems to me most worth emphasis is the nature of the psychological experience revealed. Here we have a moment of conflict between two different attitudes to life. Almost any other novelist concerned, like Butler, with 'ideas' would seize upon the situation for a battle of wits; Towneley would state his position, Ernest his. But instead we have no argument at all, merely an encounter, the words 'no, no, no', some reflections on Ernest's part and the battle is over. But it has been a battle nevertheless and one, I would suggest, more like the intellectual battles of real life both in form and significance than any number of well-turned arguments could convey.

Butler, for all the first appearances to the contrary (the hatred of the Church, the mechanical ideas of heredity, the obsession with Darwinism) was not the typical late Victorian rationalist. His philosophical position was indeed rather that of Hume:

It is faith and not logic which is the supreme arbiter. They say all roads lead to Rome, and all philosophies that I have ever seen lead ultimately either to some gross absurdity, or else to the conclusion already more than once insisted on in these pages, that the just shall live by faith, that is to say that sensible people will get through life by rule of thumb as they may interpret it most conveniently without asking too many questions for conscience's sake. Take any fact, and reason upon it to the bitter end, and it will ere long lead to this as the only refuge from some palpable folly.[10]*

Now this may not be a very satisfactory philosophy but at least it represents an emotional attitude attempting to break away from the bonds of both idealism and mechanical materialism. Butler's

* It is necessary to emphasise that this statement (in chap. LXIX) of Overton/Butler's philosophy is not a casual aside but the narrator's central comment on the central episode of the book.

'faith' is far too vague to offer anything very satisfactory in their place, but what does emerge is a healthy respect for life, a deep suspicion of idealism (reflected in the attitude to 'conscience' which Butler obviously associates with the effects of religious and anti-humanist philosophies) and a rejection (in the word 'faith') of the determinist passivity of mechanical materialism. Just what Butler's 'faith' amounts to can be judged by the total impression of *The Way of All Flesh*. Its least satisfactory side (a comparison with Hume and his game of backgammon is not irrelevant) is seen in his ultimate equating of 'sensible people' with enlightened Victorian sceptics of the bourgeois class. Hence the flatness of the last part of his novel and Mr Pritchett's feeling that 'Ernest Pontifex doesn't amount to much'. The weakness of 'common-sense' philosophy is always that common sense comes to be identified with the way of life and the particular problems of the social class one happens to live in: common sense in Ernest Pontifex's case finds its level at fifteen hundred a year. But this is not the only or the dominant impression of *The Way of All Flesh*. The most valuable and art-creating aspects of Butler's 'faith' lie in that part of his sensibility which is the most revolutionary. What is impressive about the scene between Ernest and Towneley just quoted is its revelation at one stroke both of the quality of Ernest's convictions and of their vulnerability. What Towneley brings into Ernest's dream-world is not an intellectual argument but a quality of living. That what he stands for turns out to be more trivial than Butler, perhaps, is prepared to admit, is not here the point. The excellent thing in the scene is, quite simply, its revelation of the actual processes by which the decisions of life are in fact taken. It is the kind of thing which Disraeli, for instance, never, in his novels, approaches.

But the most remarkable insight in *The Way of All Flesh* and one buried in the very heart of the book is Butler's revelation (he the intelligent Victorian bourgeois) of the final contradiction within the bourgeois dream. The section of the novel—it is its climax—in which Ernest, ill in prison, takes stock of his past and considers his future is too long to quote. It is a passage remarkable not only for its lack of sentimentality but for the profundity of its analysis of the dilemma of all intelligent and sensitive human beings in Ernest's position, and it reaches its climax in the following sentence:

It was not simply because he disliked his father and mother that he wanted to have no more to do with them; if it had been only this he would have put up with them; but a warning voice within told him distinctly enough that if he was clean cut away from them he might still have a chance of success, whereas if they had anything whatever to do with him, or even knew where he was, they would hamper him, and in the end ruin him.[11]

It is his realisation—a realisation which, on the basis of his past experience, we share—that in order to live decently, to achieve self-respect and avoid further degradation, he must cut away totally from the ties and values of the bourgeois world and his determination, on the strength of this 'warning voice', to learn a trade and change his class-allegiance; this is the most striking revelation of *The Way of All Flesh*. It is a revelation not spread glibly on the surface of the book (like some of the cracks at parsons, for instance) but forced painfully out of it and therefore in the deepest sense moving and convincing. It is interesting to compare the sentence just quoted with Butler's other remarks, already emphasised, about sensible people getting through life by rule of thumb, etc. The comparison illustrates more convincingly than any abstract argument the difference between the artistic revelation of a truth and the non-artistic statement of an idea. Butler, on one level of consciousness, did no doubt sincerely believe his Hume-like 'common-sense' philosophy which allowed him at the same time to take pot-shots at bourgeois idiocies and yet remain the bourgeois gentleman; but on another level of consciousness he knew that 'rule of thumb' could not get Ernest Pontifex out of his dilemma or fight the hated enemy. And this second level of consciousness, emerging at the climax of his novel, may without prejudice be called *deeper* than the first. For as we read *The Way of All Flesh* we know that Ernest's reactions at this moment of crisis are adequate and necessary whereas Overton/Butler's later philosophising is less than that. It is the weakness of *The Way of All Flesh* that Ernest's rebellion is frittered away (that is why the latter end of the book has so much the sense of anti-climax) but it is its strength that the decision to rebel is triumphantly reached. And you cannot separate the artistic strengths and weaknesses of the book from the strengths and weaknesses of Butler's analysis. Just in so far as Butler is able to overcome the weaknesses of his philosophical (and, in the last analysis, social) standpoint he is able to produce a work of art.

The Way of All Flesh is not, I have suggested, a moral fable. And yet in Butler's novel we have fairly continuously the sense of something being imposed on the 'life' of the story which somehow limits and flattens it: the something is Butler's opinions, his way of looking at life. And while the truth and intelligence and incisive integrity of those opinions give his book its power to stimulate us, yet the sense we have that those opinions are not wholly adequate, do not fully encompass the complexities and richness of life, this sense is the limiting factor of the book. We do not feel in *The Way of All Flesh* that Butler twists life; the world he presents to us is the real world, and it is seen with wonderful insights and yet with a certain flatness. The effect of Butler's philosophy is to make the texture of life in his novel less vibrant, less richly moving than in fact life is.

The effect in *The Way of All Flesh* of Butler's preoccupation with the moral issues of his story is to give the story this somewhat abstract flavour. We feel that the moral issues were there, so to speak, before the story. I do not think (to repeat a point previously made) that this should in any way prejudice us against the novel. What is rather odd about *The Way of All Flesh*, as novels go, is that the effect of its abstract conception is not to impose too rigid a pattern on the book but to give the book remarkably little pattern at all. In the moral fable—in *The Pilgrim's Progress,* in *Candide*, in *Hard Times*, in *The Power and the Glory*—we have something of the sense of life being put into a strait-jacket and the reason is that the moral pattern behind these books is unduly rigid—more rigid than the pattern of life. In *The Way of All Flesh* we have the opposite phenomenon: Butler's overall philosophy—that of a late-Victorian sceptical agnostic—is less rigid, more unprincipled, so to speak, than life itself and hence fails to impose a total pattern on the novel. And yet this very failure produces its own kind of rigidity. Butler's philosophy tends to *reduce* life; its effect on his book is precisely the same.

One would not wish to end on a negative note. *The Way of All Flesh* is a remarkable and invigorating novel and one which, in the 1870s, it was deeply necessary to write. One has only to compare it with, say, *Adam Bede* (1859) or *Barchester Towers* (1857) to appreciate the quality not merely of Butler's ideas but of his art. The necessities behind the book, the insistent, fearless attacks on the shams and false values of the Victorian bourgeoisie, are not side-issues or eccentricities and Butler's hard, urbane, yet unadorned prose derives its vitality from the sheer mental courage of his penetration into the myths and complacencies of his class. His book triumphantly carries onwards that function of the novel which the eighteenth-century writers all emphasised—the destruction of romance.

4

THOMAS HARDY: TESS OF THE D'URBERVILLES

(1891)

The subject of *Tess of the D'Urbervilles* is stated clearly by Hardy to be the fate of a 'pure woman'; in fact it is the destruction of the English peasantry. More than any other nineteenth-century novel we have touched on it has the quality of a social document. It has even, for all its high-pitched emotional quality, the kind of impersonality that the expression suggests. Its subject is all-pervasive, affecting and determining the nature of every part. It is a novel with a thesis—a *roman à thèse*—and the thesis is true.

The thesis is that in the course of the nineteenth century the disintegration of the peasantry—a process which had its roots deep in the past—had reached its final and tragic stage. With the extension of capitalist farming (farming, that is to say, in which the landowner farms not for sustenance but for profit and in which the land-workers become wage-earners) the old yeoman class of small-holders or peasants, with their traditions of independence and their own native culture, was bound to disappear. The developing forces of history were too strong for them and their way of life. And because that way of life had been proud and deep-rooted its destruction was necessarily painful and tragic. *Tess* is the story and the symbol of the destruction.

Tess Durbeyfield is a peasant girl. Her parents belong to a class ranking above the farm-labourers, a class 'including the carpenter, the smith, the shoemaker, the huckster, together with nondescript workers other than farm-labourers; a set of people who owed a certain stability of aim and conduct to the fact of their being life-holders, like Tess's father, or copy-holders, or, occasionally, small

freeholders'.[1] Already by the opening of the novel the Durbeyfields
have fallen on hard times, a plight by no means solely due to the
lack of stability in the characters of John and Joan. A further twist
is given to their difficulty in making ends meet by the accident in
which their horse is killed.* It is her sense of guilt over this accident
that allows Tess to be persuaded by her mother into visiting the
Trantridge D'Urbervilles to 'claim kin' with a more prosperous
branch of the family. And from this visit (itself an attempt to solve
the Durbeyfields' economic problems) the whole tragedy derives.

In these opening chapters of the novel there is an immediate and
insistent emphasis on historical processes, so that from the start
the characters are not seen merely as individuals. The discovery by
John Durbeyfield of his ancestry is not just an introductory comic
scene, a display of quaint 'character'. It states the basic theme of
the novel—what the Durbeyfields have been and what they
become. The landscape in the second chapter (it is far more effective
description than the famous set-piece at the beginning of *The
Return of the Native*) is described and given significance almost
wholly in terms of history. The 'club-walking' scene, again, is
contrasted with the May Day dances of the past and early pagan
rites are recalled. Tess is revealed as one of a group, typical ('not
handsomer than others'[2]), and in the comparison between her and
her mother the differences brought about by historical changes are
emphasised. Joan Durbeyfield lives in the peasant folk-lore of the
past, Tess has been to a National school. 'When they were together
the Jacobean and the Victorian ages were juxtaposed.'[3]

The sacrifice of Tess to D'Urberville is symbolic of the historical
process at work. D'Urberville is not, of course, a D'Urberville at
all, but the son of the *nouveau riche* Stoke family, capitalists who
have bought their way into the gentry, and Tess's cry when she
sees the D'Urberville estate: 'I thought we were an old family; but
this is all new!'[4] carries a world of irony. Tess herself does not want
to go to D'Urberville's and when she does finally agree to go she
dresses in her working clothes. But her mother insists on her
dressing up for the occasion.

---

* This very accident is a striking symbol of the struggles of the peasantry. The
mail-cart 'with its two noiseless wheels, speeding along these lanes like an arrow' runs
into Tess's slow, unlighted wagon. Anyone who happened to be in Italy during the
last war will recall the running-down of peasant carts by army vehicles. The army
drivers were not always to blame. The peasants as often as not had no lights and were
on the wrong side of the road. But every accident represented a clash between something more than two individual vehicles and the results in hardship or worse can well
be imagined.

'Very well; I suppose you know,' replied Tess with calm abandonment. And to please her parent the girl put herself quite in Joan's hands, saying serenely, 'Do what you like with me, Mother.'[5]

Again the moment is symbolic. Tess, prepared to become, since change she must, a worker, is handed over by her mother to the life and the mercies of the ruling class.

From the moment of her seduction by D'Urberville, Tess's story becomes a hopeless struggle, against overwhelming odds, to maintain her self-respect. After the death of her child she becomes a wage-labourer at the dairy-farm at Talbothays. The social degradation is mitigated by the kindness of the dairyman and his wife, but the work is only seasonal. Here however she meets and falls in love with Angel Clare and through marriage to him thinks to escape her fate. But Angel, the intellectual, turns out to be more cruel than D'Urberville, the sensualist. Angel, with all his emancipated ideas, is not merely a prig and a hypocrite but a snob as well. He understands nothing of the meaning of the decline of the D'Urbervilles and his attitude to Tess is one of self-righteous idealisation.

'My position—is this,' he said abruptly. 'I thought—any man would have thought—that by giving up all ambition to win a wife with social standing, with fortune, with knowledge of the world, I should secure rustic innocence as surely as I should secure pink cheeks. . . .'[6]

And when his dream of rustic innocence is shattered he can only taunt Tess with:

'Don't, Tess; don't argue. Different societies, different manners. You almost make me say you are an unapprehending peasant woman, who have never been initiated into the proportions of social things. . . .'[7]

Even at the moment of her deepest humiliation Tess is stung to the retort:

'Lots of families are as bad as mine in that! Retty's family were once large landowners, and so were Dairyman Billett's. And the Debbyhouses, who now are carters, were once the De Bayeux family. You find such as I everywhere; 'tis a feature of the country, and I can't help it.'[8]

It is important (I shall return to this point) to give these passages their full weight because they emphasise the kind of novel this is. Such passages, read as 'psychological drama', ring queer and unconvincing. Their function in the novel is to stress the social nature of Tess's destiny and its typicality.

After Angel has left her the social degradation of Tess continues. At the farm at Flintcomb Ash she and the other girls (once again it is significant that Tess's fate is shared by Marion and Izz who have not, in the same way, 'sinned' morally) become fully proletarianised, working for wages in the hardest, most degrading conditions. The scene at the threshing is here particularly important, a symbol of the dehumanised relationships of the new capitalist farms. At Talbothays there had at least been some possibility of pride and interest in the labour as well as a certain kindliness in the common kitchen at which the dairyman's wife presided. Here there is nothing kind or satisfying and the emphasis on Marion's bottle is not casual, not just a matter of the individual 'character'.

The final blow to Tess's attempts to maintain her self-respect comes with the death of her father and the consequent expulsion of the Durbeyfields from their cottage. John Durbeyfield had been a life-holder:

But as the long holdings fell in they were seldom again let to similar tenants, and were mostly pulled down, if not absolutely required by the farmer for his hands. Cottagers who were not directly employed on the land were looked upon with disfavour, and the banishment of some starved the trade of others, who were thus obliged to follow. These families, who had formed the backbone of the village life in the past, who were the depositories of the village traditions, had to seek refuge in the large centres; the process, humorously designated by statisticians as 'the tendency of the rural population towards the large towns', being really the tendency of water to flow uphill when forced by machinery.[9]

It is the need to support her family, thus driven off the land, that finally forces Tess back to Alec D'Urberville. And when Angel, chastened and penitent, returns, the final sacrifice is inevitable. Tess kills D'Urberville. The policemen take her from the altar at Stonehenge and the black flag is run up on Winchester jail.

It is important for a number of reasons to emphasise that *Tess of the D'Urbervilles* is a moral fable, that it is the expression of a generalised human situation in history and neither (what it is generally assumed to be) a purely personal tragedy nor (what Hardy appears to have intended) a philosophic comment on Life in general and the fate of Woman in particular. If we read the novel as a personal tragedy, the individual history of Tess Durbeyfield, a great deal strikes us as extremely unsatisfactory.

In the first place there is (as has been noted frequently enough) Hardy's flouting of normal probability in his insistence on a series of the most unlucky chances. In *Tess* the most notable of these chances are the episode in which Tess's written confession, pushed under Angel's door, goes under the carpet and the moment when Tess, having walked from Flintcomb Ash to Emminster, overhears Angel's brothers talking about her and has not the heart to visit her parents-in-law. If either of these chance happenings had not occurred, all might easily have been saved. Again, in the broader realm of probability, is there really any adequate reason why Tess, at the end, should murder D'Urberville? True, she does not know the full extent of Angel's forgiveness, but at least she knows that he has basically changed. It is not perhaps any one of these manifestations of tragic improbability that we are likely to jib at, but rather the combination of them. Mr J. I. M. Stewart, in an interesting essay, has stated the problem.

Always in Hardy it is certain that the incidence of fatality within the general operation of chance will be higher than we are commonly prepared to accept of its being in nature. Why does he thus so often seem to play against his characters with loaded dice; why does he darken the sky with his arrows when Elfride Swancourt and her many successors are fighting for life? The universe of his novels is one of a determinism slightly modified to meet the needs of tragedy, the individual will being conceived as having its measure of freedom during certain moments of equilibrium in the universal Will, within which it is comprised (the image is Hardy's). It is thus still a *neutral* universe. Why then does the screw turn so frequently and so disastrously as it does?[10]

Now if we read the novel as a detailed particularised study of an individual life it is clear that this turning of the screw does constitute a serious weakness. What it amounts to in *Tess* is that we must regard the characters—Tess herself in particular—as having less than normal luck and—more important—less than normal human resilience in the situation in which they find themselves. Is not Tess, after all (admitting her superiority of sensitiveness), a good deal less shrewd and wordly-wise than a peasant girl of her age might naturally be assumed to be? Is not her very sensitiveness a little false? (Could she, for instance, have *afforded*—bearing in mind the conditions of Flintcomb Ash—to be merely hurt and un-protesting when Angel's brothers take away her boots when they find them in the ditch?) Such considerations are, if the novel is a realistic psychological study, entirely relevant. But they seem to me,

in fact, no more relevant than the criticism which says of *King
Lear* that Lear's conduct in the first act is unlikely or that the
Gloucester sub-plot is ill-planned because the existence of two
such cases of filial impiety within so small a circumference is improbable. *Tess* is not a novel of the kind of *Emma* or *Middlemarch*.
It does not illuminate within a detailed framework particular
problems of human conduct and feeling. Its sphere is the more
generalised movement of human destiny.

Once we recognise that the subject of *Tess* is the destruction of
the peasantry many of the more casual criticisms of the book are
seen to be rather wide of the mark.

There is the question, for instance, of Alec D'Urberville. Many
readers are antagonised by his presentation as what amounts to the
stock villain of Victorian melodrama, the florid, moustache-twirling
bounder who refers to the heroine (whom he is about to seduce) as
'Well, my Beauty . . .'. Is this not a character who has stepped direct
out of the tenth-rate theatre or 'She was poor but she was honest'?
It seems to me that almost the whole point about D'Urberville is
that he is indeed the archetypal Victorian villain. Far from being
weakened by the associations of crude melodrama he in fact
illuminates the whole type and we understand better *why* the
character of which he is a symbol did dominate a certain grade of
Victorian entertainment and was enthusiastically hissed by the
audience. It is the very typicality of D'Urberville that serves the
purposes of the novel.

The treatment of Christianity in the book has a similar relevance.
The conversion of D'Urberville is not in itself necessary
to the plot of the novel (his rediscovery of Tess could easily
have been contrived some other way). Hardy's object here is
clearly to heighten the association, implicit throughout the book,
of the Christian faith and Tess's downfall. The man with the
paint-pot who regales Tess with the assurance that THY DAMNATION
SLUMBERETH NOT at the moment of her betrayal turns up again
with the converted D'Urberville. Is the comment fair to Christianity? The question is not relevant. Hardy is not attempting an
estimate of the total validity of the Christian philosophy. His subject
is the destruction of the peasant Tess. It is the place of religious
influence in that destruction that is his concern. And in the pattern
of the novel the Christian church is seen as at best a neutral observer,
at worst an active abettor in the process of destruction. It is not,
historically considered, an unreasonable comment.

At best a neutral observer, at worst an active abettor: the phrase applies to a good deal more than Hardy's view of Christianity. One of the aspects of *Tess* that we tend to find peculiarly un-convincing—if not repulsive—is the sense of the loaded dice to which Mr Stewart refers. It emerges in its least palatable form in passages of the book most obviously intended as fundamental philosophical comment. There is the famous episode, for instance, in which Tess, driving the cart to market, speaks to her little brother of the stars:

'Did you say the stars were worlds, Tess?'
'Yes.'
'All like ours?'
'I don't know; but I think so. They sometimes seem to be like the apples on our stubbard-tree. Most of them splendid and sound—a few blighted.'
'Which do we live on—a splendid one or a blighted one?'
'A blighted one.'
'Tis very unlucky that we didn't pitch on a sound one, when there were so many more of 'em!'
'Yes.'
'Is it like that really, Tess?' said Abraham, turning to her much im-pressed, on reconsideration of this rare information. 'How would it have been if we had pitched on a sound one?'
'Well, Father wouldn't have coughed and creeped about as he does, and wouldn't have got too tipsy to go this journey; and Mother wouldn't have been always washing, and never getting finished.'
'And you would have been a rich lady ready-made, and not have had to be made rich by marrying a gentleman?'
'O Aby, don't—don't talk of that any more!'[11]

We tend to reject such an episode on two grounds: in the first place we are not convinced that any peasant girl would talk like that, in the second the philosophy implied (and the whole organisation of the book makes us give it the weight of the author's full sympathy, if not assent) is not calculated to win our support. The world as a blighted apple is an image too facile to satisfy us, even though we may recognise the force of Tess's pessimism. I think it is important, however, to emphasise that even in this passage the pessimism is given a very explicit basis in actual conditions. It is the kind of life her parents lead that drives Tess to her feelings of despair and it is the sentence about her mother never getting finished that in fact saves the scene. For here is no pretentious philosophy of fatality but a bitterly realistic recalling of the actual fate of millions of working women.

The scene just quoted seems to me to give a most instructive insight into the kind of book *Tess of the D'Urbervilles* is. It is not, it has already been emphasised, a 'psychological novel'; the presentation of Tess's actual thoughts in this episode is not at all convincing. Nor is it a symbolic statement on the level of *Wuthering Heights*; Hardy does not penetrate to the profundity of Emily Brontë's understanding of the processes of life and when he goes in for philosophical generalisations the result is often embarrassing. And yet this novel, with its queer cramped 'literary' style* and its bogus 'Aeschylean' philosophy, gets hold of something of life and illuminates a phase of human history with an extraordinary compulsion and an insight of oddly moving delicacy.

What Hardy got hold of was not, I think, quite what his conscious mind believed. In the scene we have just discussed the *intention* (as opposed to the total effect) is to concentrate into the image of the blighted star a whole world of philosophical significance. Hardy took his philosophy of the Immanent Will very seriously and undoubtedly saw Tess as the victim of 'the President of the Immortals'. A pessimistic and determinist view of the world in which man (and, even more, woman) is at the mercy of an unyielding outside Fate is the conscious philosophy behind the novel. The sub-title 'a pure woman' is indicative of the kind of significance Hardy gave to his story, and there is no doubt that this conscious philosophy affects the book, in general for the worse. It is responsible, for instance, for the 'literary' quality which mars the final sentence. It is responsible for our sense of loaded dice. And it is responsible ultimately for the psychological weakness such as the idealisation of Tess, for the characters are made too often to respond not to life but to Hardy's philosophy.†

And yet *Tess* survives Hardy's philosophy. It survives because his imaginative understanding of the disintegration of the peasantry is more powerful than the limiting tendencies of his conscious outlook. As a matter of fact I do not think we ought to sneer too securely at Hardy's philosophy. No doubt it is, like Tolstoy's, an unsatisfactory philosophy and yet also, like Tolstoy's (the views of history expressed in *War and Peace* and *The Dynasts* are worth

---

* 'When [Hardy] remarked that had he known what a stir *Tess* was going to create he would have made it a really good book he probably meant that he would have gone over the grammar, and would have inserted more of those references to mythology or painting that he believed an important means of toning up a literary style.'[12] Mr. Stewart's comment seems to me fair enough.

† All three of these qualities are combined in the dreadful moment when Angel, at the very climax of the book, after Tess's confession of her 'sin', exclaims: 'My God—how can forgiveness meet such a grotesque—prestidigitation as that!'[13]

comparing) it emerges from a passionately honest attempt to grapple with real problems of quite overwhelming difficulty. Hardy at least did have a philosophy (which is more than can be said for most of his contemporaries) and there was more basis to his pessimism—the pessimism of the Wessex peasant who sees his world and his values being destroyed—than can be laughed away with an easy gesture of contempt.

For the odd thing about this strange and moving novel is that although so much about it has a note of falsity—the manipulation of the plot, the character-study of Tess herself, the inadequate, self-conscious, stilted writing—the total impression is not false at all. Part of the achievement is due undoubtedly to the always effective and often superb evocation of the natural background. This is a special triumph of Hardy's and one which—in the novels we have previously discussed—had hitherto scarcely been attempted. Such a description as that of the dawn at Talbothays may perhaps best be compared with the descriptions of London in *Oliver Twist*. In neither case is the word 'descriptive', with its cold suggestion of an objective backcloth, adequate.

They met continually; they could not help it. They met daily in that strange and solemn interval, the twilight of the morning, in the violet or pink dawn; for it was necessary to rise early, so very early, here. Milking was done betimes; and before the milking came the skimming, which began a little past three. It usually fell to the lot of some one or other of them to wake the rest, the first being aroused by an alarm-clock; and, as Tess was the latest arrival, and they soon discovered that she could be depended upon not to sleep through the alarm as the others did, this task was thrust most frequently upon her. No sooner had the hour of three struck and whizzed, than she left her room and ran to the dairyman's door; then up the ladder to Angel's, calling him in a loud whisper; then woke her fellow-milkmaids. By the time that Tess was dressed Clare was downstairs and out in the humid air. The remaining maids and the dairyman usually gave themselves another turn on the pillow, and did not appear till a quarter of an hour later.

The grey half-tones of daybreak are not the grey half-tones of the day's close, though the degree of their shade may be the same. In the twilight of the morning light seems active, darkness passive; in the twilight of evening it is the darkness which is active and crescent, and light which is the drowsy reverse. . . .

At these non-human hours they could get quite close to the waterfowl. Herons came, with a great bold noise as of opening doors and shutters, out of the boughs of a plantation which they frequented at the side of the mead; or, if already on the spot, hardily maintained their standing in the water as the pair walked by, watching them by moving their heads round in a slow, horizontal, passionless wheel, like the turn of puppets by clockwork.

They could then see the faint summer fogs in layers, woolly, level, and apparently no thicker than counterpanes, spread about the meadows in detached remnants of small extent. On the grey moisture of the grass were marks where the cows had lain through the night—dark-green islands of dry herbage the size of their carcases, in the general sea of dew. From each island proceeded a serpentine trail, by which the cow had rambled away to feed after getting up, at the end of which trail they found her; the snoring puff from her nostrils, when she recognised them, making an intenser little fog of her own amid the prevailing one. Then they drove the animals back to the barton, or sat down to milk them on the spot, as the case might require.

Or perhaps the summer fog was more general, and the meadows lay like a white sea, out of which the scattered trees rose like dangerous rocks. Birds would soar through it into the upper radiance, and hang on the wing sunning themselves, or alight on the wet rails subdividing the mead, which now shone like glass rods. Minute diamonds of moisture from the mist hung, too, upon Tess's eyelashes and drops upon her hair, like seed pearls. When the day grew quite strong and commonplace these dried off her; moreover, Tess then lost her strange and etherial beauty; her teeth, lips, and eyes scintillated in the sunbeams, and she was again the dazzlingly fair dairymaid only, who had to hold her own against the other women of the world.[14]

The atmosphere evoked in such description is not an embellishment to the book, but an integral part of it. We cannot think of Tess and Angel except in the context of such scenes any more than we can think of Sikes outside the context of the London which has made him. We believe in Tess, just as we believe in Sikes, because her relationship to her world is so successfully conveyed. When Hardy begins theorising, discussing in abstract terms Tess's plight, we become uneasy; when he presents her to us in the misty dawn at Talbothays we feel no need to question her authenticity.* She *is* a peasant girl and she *is* splendid, heroic even, and we know what

---

* D. H. Lawrence in his 'Study of Thomas Hardy' wrote:

'. . . it is not as a metaphysician that we must consider Hardy. He makes a poor show there. For nothing in his work is so pitiable as his clumsy efforts to push events into line with his theory of being, and to make calamity fall on those who represent the principle of Love. . . .

'His feeling, his instinct, his sensuous understanding is, however, apart from his metaphysic, very great and deep, deeper than that, perhaps, of any other English novelist. Putting aside his metaphysic, which must always obtrude when he thinks of people, and turning to the earth, to landscape, then he is true to himself.' *Phoenix* (1936), p. 980.

Hardy means when he talks of 'a pure woman'. The unconvincing moments are those when to make a 'point' Hardy allows his own, inadequate *ideas* to weaken his profound instinctive *understanding*. Such a moment arises when, just before Tess's confession to Angel, he too is made to confess a sexual lapse. Now Hardy can convince us that Angel is a prig and a hypocrite but he simply cannot convince us that the Angel he presents to us in the novel would be quite so morally obtuse as to see no affinity whatever between his confession and hers. He might well convince us that a man only slightly less morally aware would be thus blinded (heaven knows the situation is common enough). He might even convince us that Angel himself would be capable of putting a youthful indiscretion into a separate compartment of his mind and there burying it. But to ask us to believe that the Angel we know (and one is not claiming of course any very admirable qualities for him) would within a few minutes of confessing such a lapse of his own respond in quite the way he does to Tess's confession is simply asking us to stretch our credulity beyond its limit. And the reason for it all is obvious. Hardy is determined at all costs to make his point (fair enough in the abstract) about male hypocrisy on this sexual matter. He is determined to get in another blow on behalf of his pure woman. But, because the moral point is unconvincingly realised in this particular scene between these particular characters, the blow rebounds.

It is not, of course, a fatal error (there are far graver difficulties in the book) but I quote it to illustrate the battle going on throughout *Tess* between Hardy's ideas and his understanding. It is the inadequacy of his ideas that gives much of the book its oddly thin and stilted quality and which leads, in particular, to the unsatisfactory manipulation of chance which, more than anything in the novel, arouses our suspicions as to its validity. For the loading of the dice is an admission not so much of cunning as of impotence, a desperate gesture which attempts through artificial stimulation to achieve a consummation otherwise unobtainable. Hardy's understanding, his deep instinctive comprehension of the fate of the Wessex peasants, told him what had to be said, but his conscious philosophy did not give him adequate means always to say it. Hence the unduly long arm of coincidence, hence the half-digested classical allusions, hence the psychological weaknesses. Whereas from the social understanding emerges the strength of the novel, the superb revelation of the relation of men to nature, the haunting evocation of the Wessex landscape not as backcloth but as the living challenging material of human existence, and the profoundly moving story of the peasant Tess.

It is easy enough to list the imperfections of this novel. What also needs explanation is its triumph, epitomised in that extraordinary final scene at Stonehenge. There is nothing bogus about the achievement here, no sleight of hand, no counterfeit notes of false emotion. The words of speech have not quite the ring of speech nor the integral force of poetry; the symbolism is obvious, one might almost say crude. And yet this very clumsiness, the almost amateurish manipulation of the mechanics of the scene, contributes something to its force, to its expression of the pathetic and yet heroic losing battle waged by Tess against a world she cannot successfully fight and can only dimly apprehend. The final mood evoked by *Tess of the D'Urbervilles* is not hopelessness but indignation and the indignation is none the less profound for being incompletely intellectualised. Hardy is not a Shakespeare or an Emily Brontë. His art does not quite achieve that sense of the inner movement of life which transcends abstractions. He is constantly weakening his apprehension of this movement by inadequate attitudes and judgements. But in spite of this weakening *Tess* emerges as a fine novel, a moral fable, the most moving expression in our literature—not forgetting Wordsworth—of the destruction of the peasant world.*

* For a further assessment of *Tess* involving some modification of the above see my Introduction to the Standard Edition of *Tess of the D'Urbervilles* (New York, Harper and Row, 1966).

PART II
The Twentieth Century:
The First Quarter

I

INTRODUCTION

With Conrad we are in the twentieth century. It is not merely a question of the dates of publication: it is a whole historical vista that has changed. The world of *Nostromo* is the world of modern imperialism, of war and violence and concentration camps, of displaced persons and mass neurosis, all on a scale and of a kind radically different from previous human experience. The disintegration of Victorian bourgeois society has reached a further stage, the stage imaginatively envisaged in *Wuthering Heights*, in which the polite veils of conduct and assumption have been removed, and tensions and conflicts acquire the urgency and directness of mass warfare, unimagined economic crisis and the revolutionary clash of opposing classes.

It is not surprising to find that the prevailing tone of twentieth-century English literature, from whatever point of view it may be written, is one of uncertainty and tension. Even in the gentlest novelists, the most urbane and apparently detached, E. M. Forster and Virginia Woolf, there is a deep sense of strain and insecurity.

It is generally assumed that the great complexity of modern life and the sense of flux and uncertainty of a revolutionary period make writing unusually·difficult. Certainly the general condition of English culture in the last fifty years would seem at first glance to bear out this thesis.

It cannot possibly be our object to analyse here or to discuss fully so complicated and difficult a situation. Rather than offer a number of generalised conclusions which it would be impossible in a short space to substantiate, I would wish merely to indicate some of the main issues involved.

(1) The most striking and in some respects the most alarming feature in the development of the novel in the twentieth century has been the ever-increasing separation between the 'good' and the 'popular'. On the one hand the majority of the novels most highly praised and valued by the intellectual arbiters are almost entirely unread by the mass of the people (this was not so in the days of Scott or Dickens); on the other hand both the middle-brow best seller and the mass-produced reading material of the majority of the people is despised and almost unread by the intellectuals. The consequences of this situation, like its causes, are numerous. Not merely has the commercialisation of literature had a disastrous effect on the general reading standards of the public, but the 'good' writer has come to be a more and more lonely and isolated figure, exploring a very limited range of experience for the benefit of a small audience of similarly placed admirers. Among the results is that 'good' literature is (not unfairly) associated in the minds of millions with obscurity, affectation and all the intellectual and social snobbery of high-browism, while popularity has ceased to be an issue with the majority of serious writers and is even regarded with suspicion and contempt.

(2) Thus relieved from the obligation of writing literature which is in any sense of the word popular, the tendency of writers born into or acquiring the habits of the middle-class intelligentsia has been to explore with an ever more obsessive intensity small specialised areas of their peculiar, and generally quite *atypical*, sensibility. The theories of both Freudian and Jungian psychology have further encouraged this tendency, as have certain aspects of the writings of Dostoievsky and Proust and the remarkable and perverse achievement of Kafka. The sense of isolation of the artist-intellectual in contemporary society reaches its climax in Kafka's work in which nightmare becomes reality and the individual is trapped in a world, not merely hostile to him personally, but apparently impervious to human action. Extremes of pessimism, neurosis, and despair have become the accepted attitudes behind a considerable proportion of serious literature.

(3) In even the greatest writers of the age—Conrad, Lawrence, Joyce—the battle of the novelist with his raw material tends to be an unequal one. None of these writers tamely accepts the decadent aspects of the society in which they all find themselves, yet not one of them is able to achieve a philosophy and hence an artistic

vantage-point from which he is able quite satisfactorily to cope with and subjugate the world he tackles. Hence, for all the brilliance, the sense of strain, the lack of confident relaxation (the relaxation of a Fielding or a Tolstoy), the excessive intensity and the constant tendency to topple over the verge of sanity into mistiness or obscurity or hysteria.

(4) Side by side with the books which we shall consider in the following pages there have appeared during this century a number of novels, of varying merit, written from a fundamentally different point of view, that of the working class as such. It is impossible in a work planned along the present lines to give these novels the discussion they deserve; simply to include one or two of them alongside a totally different type of writing would be satisfactory from no point of view. It must suffice merely to mention Robert Tressall's *The Ragged Trousered Philanthropists* (1914) and Lewis Grassic Gibbon's *A Scots Quair* (1932–4) as important and moving novels which have to be seen in their historical context as the beginning of something new in our literature. Unlike the bulk of the novels discussed in this volume they do not belong to the end of an epoch.

(5) In the first half of the twentieth century the long battle of the English novel towards a full and all-inclusive realism becomes, all too often, sidetracked. As the issues become more violent and extreme the struggle to see life steadily and whole becomes more and more difficult and taxing. To quote Maxim Gorky: 'Most people think and argue not in order to investigate the phenomena of life but rather because they are in a hurry to find a quiet haven for their thoughts and to establish all sorts of "undisputed truths".' I would suggest that the main problem facing the twentieth-century writer is not the nature of his raw material but the difficulty of achieving a standpoint from which vital experience can be defined, organised and controlled. There is no particular reason for believing that good art cannot emerge from a period of great social and spiritual change. On the contrary there are historical and common-sense grounds for supposing that such a period should be particularly rich in artistic possibilities.

2

JOSEPH CONRAD: NOSTROMO

(1904)

The first and immediate impression that *Nostromo* makes upon the reader comes from the strength and luxuriance of Conrad's descriptive writing. The evocation of the Republic of Costaguana—an entire South American state whose political and social history over a number of years is the subject of the novel—is astonishingly concrete, not merely rich and colourful but solid in a way no mere piling up of adjectives can achieve. It is worth emphasising right away the purpose of this evocation and the means by which it is achieved.

It is essential to Conrad's intention that there should be no dubiety about the setting of his novel. The relationship between background and characters must be fully and unambiguously established. The descriptive backcloth to *Nostromo* such as the opening chapter, is not a collection of purple passages, vaguely romantic, prose equivalents of 'glorious technicolor'. The very first sentence is significant:

In the time of Spanish rule, and for many years afterwards, the town of Sulaco—the luxuriant beauty of the orange gardens bears witness to its antiquity—had never been commercially anything more important than a coasting port with a fairly large local trade in ox-hides and indigo.

The colour is there—the orange gardens, the ox-hides and the indigo—but the body of the sentence is concerned with the issues that are to be the main subjects of the novel: government and trade. Conrad's purpose is to establish a solid background because this is a solid novel, a novel about the real world, about a particular republic in a particular part of the world at a particular epoch in history. Without the ability to make peculiarly concrete the scenes and settings of his story that combination of outward clarity and inward depth which is one of Conrad's characteristics would be lost. For this novelist (and we shall have to return to the point), though he is not a superficial writer, though his characters have an 'inwardness' in something of the way of Dostoievsky's or James's people, is yet concerned essentially with the real, material world. One never gets from his books the impression that the inner life, intensely and indeed supremely important as it is, is *more real* than, or in some way quite isolated from, the physical world. I make this point because there are two tendencies in critical attitudes towards Conrad, both of which seem to me disastrously wrong: on the one hand is the emphasis on the qualities of sheer glamour and action in his books, the view which sees him as 'the Kipling of the Seas'; on the other is the tendency to associate him with the twentieth-century cult of isolation and despair, to make of him so to speak —a sort of archetypal 'displaced person' with all the implications that such a status involves.

Some kind of 'moral discovery', Conrad wrote, 'should be the object of every tale'.[1] He was no Art-for-Arter, this artist who, incredibly, wrote his books in a foreign language which he learned as an adult, and wrestled with his novels in a way reminiscent of Flaubert, the novelist whom he most admired. And by 'moral discovery' he did not mean merely the illustration of some pre-conceived moral truth. It was in the creation of the work of art that the discovery was made. This seems to me very important. The very act of artistic creation, that moulding into significant form of some thing or part of life, is in itself a discovery about the nature of life and ultimately its value will lie in the value of that discovery. It is interesting, incidentally, that illuminating remarks about his art come more frequently in the novels themselves than in his prefaces which are oddly naïve and unsatisfactory. The explanation undoubtedly lies in this word 'discovery'. It was in his artistic grappling with life, not in his logical thinking about it, that Conrad delved deepest and with best result.

What were the 'moral discoveries' he made? It is not easy to define them because he never did so himself. In fact when he tried he is disappointing. 'What is so elusive about him,' Mr E. M. Forster has excellently said,

'is that he is always promising to make some general philosophic statement about the universe, and then refraining with a gruff disclaimer. . . .

No creed, in fact. Only opinions and the right to throw them overboard when facts make them look absurd. Opinions held under the semblance of eternity, girt with the sea, crowned with the stars, and therefore easily mistaken for a creed.[2]

That seems to get him: no creed, but an unflinching respect for facts, the facts of the world he lived in. The moral discoveries are always based on facts.

The most important fact of all to Conrad is the social nature of man. It is a fact (or, if you will, an opinion based on fact) which permeates his books and informs, not least, that hard and 'jewelled' style, generally so concrete in its imagery, so controlled in its movement.

Conrad began writing in the eighteen-nineties, after twenty years as a sailor and adventurer. His early books are nearly all about the sea or about distant lands: Malaya, Indonesia, India, Africa. What were the 'facts' he found? Not merely, as some of his admirers would pretend, glamour, adventure, colour, romance. There is an uglier word as well: imperialism. Conrad doesn't use the word; clearly it wasn't part of his familiar vocabulary. What is significant is that at this period when the growth of imperialism was the dominant factor (or fact) in world history, only two considerable writers of English—Kipling and Conrad—looked this phenomenon in the face. From their experience both of them gained a vitality which other writers of their age notably lacked. But only Conrad looked at imperialism honestly enough to become a great artist.

'There is a taint of death, a flavour of mortality in lies—which is exactly what I hate and detest in the world,' he wrote in *Heart of Darkness*, perhaps the most horrifying description of the effects of imperialism ever written. While Kipling celebrated the white man's burden Conrad wrote what he saw. He is describing Stein in *Lord Jim*:

There were very few places in the Archipelago he had not seen in the original dusk of their being, before light (even electric light) had been carried into them for the sake of better morality and—and—well—the greater profit, too. . . .[3]

The hesitancy will out, but so will the moral discovery. For all his temperamental conservatism, all his loyalty to Britain and its Empire, his honesty time and again wins through. None of his stories is propagandist. He will not sell himself. His feeling for the native peoples is sincere. Dain Warris in *Lord Jim*, Hassim in *The Rescue* are presented with the greatest sympathy and dignity, indeed they are among Conrad's few characters (apart from the women) who can be said to be idealised. And the truth is that these young Malayan aristocrats are conceived as Polish rather than Malayan nationalists. They are not among Conrad's successes because, excusably, for all his sympathy he did not understand these people.

As he grew older the moral discoveries he drew from his art became rather more fully rationalised. His hatred of financial speculation (what he calls 'material interests') may be an opinion rather than a creed, but it is an opinion which permeates several of the later novels. *Chance* is full of it. Marlow's descriptions of the financial dealings of de Barral is a splendid piece of ironic writing equalled by the scorn bestowed on the Tropical Coal Belt Company in *Victory*. But to abstract single themes from particular novels is a dangerous practice and can easily be a misleading one. I wish merely to emphasise that Conrad's concern with imperialism is no chance interest but is central to his whole work which is the presentation through his art of man as a social being.

Nostromo, a Tale of the Seaboard as it is inadequately described by its author, is a political novel in the widest sense, the sense in which Aristotle and Marx use the word politics. Its background is the history of a South American republic—presented, as I have already suggested, with extraordinary concreteness—that passes through a revolution which establishes a liberal parliamentarian régime, a counter-revolution led by totally unprincipled adventurers and a third revolution which (in the particular province concerned) re-establishes the liberals. The liberals—bourgeois parliamentarians distinguishable from the counter-revolutionaries principally by a greater smoothness of manners—are supported and financed by the owners of the greatest power in the land, the San Tomé silver mine, run by an Englishman, Charles Gould, backed by American capital. The main theme of the novel, fundamental to the personal themes that form the 'story', is the corrupting power of the silver mine which changes all that touches it—dehumanises Gould and dries up his marriage, makes a mockery of the liberal ideals of the parliamentarians and the Christianity of the American capitalist, corrupts the incorruptible Nostromo, Capataz de Cargadores, great man of the People, symbol of their aspirations.

Nostromo is, from the technical point of view, an amazing *tour*

de force. The method Conrad uses is of particular interest because
his problems are the characteristic problems of the modern novelist
—to present a wide canvas in which essentials are not lost in too
great detail; to convey political and social movement on various
levels (conscious, unconscious, semi-conscious); to suggest the
almost infinite inter-relatedness of character and character, character
and background; to give each character a real individuality and yet
see each as part of a concrete whole: in short, to show men in
society. Conrad's method is to over-simplify somewhat individual
character in the sense of giving each individual very sharply-
defined personal characteristics, frequently reiterated, so that each
stands out clearly, not only in contrast to the others, but against
the clear, concrete, surface-objective background of the whole.
Thus the girl Antonia is invariably associated with a fan, Nostromo
with silver and the epithet 'illustrious', Dr Monygham with a lame
leg, a twisted body and scarred cheeks, the Garibaldino with his
'mane' (it is, in a sense, the old 'humours' theory developed poetically). What at first appears a somewhat irritating insistence is seen
after a time to be a conscious and essential method. In fact, of
course, the characters are not simple at all: by the end of the book
their depths and complexities are well established; it is their
presentation which is simplified. Like the Elizabethan dramatists,
Conrad employs his own convention for the revelation of social
life. Just as Hamlet is at once a type and an individual, the melan-
cholic, conventionally presented in a way the audience immediately
grasps, and gradually revealed in all his complexity and significance,
so is Monygham, the cynical but austere moralist, conventionally
presented to the reader with his scarred face and twisted body and
—thus immediately apprehended in essentials—plays his part in
the vivid pattern of the novel, while the full depth and significance
of his character is gradually revealed. One might contrast Conrad's
method, highly conventionalised and dependent on a continuously
controlled and (in a wholly laudatory sense) artificial prose, with
that of John Dos Passos who, twenty years later, in an even more
ambitious political novel, *U.S.A.*, achieves breadth only at the
sacrifice of depth and a colloquial prose style at the sacrifice of all
reasonable brevity.

I will give one example of the method of *Nostromo*, a passage
following a scene of great intimacy between Antonia, the daughter
of the idealist liberal leader, and Decoud, the sceptical, unprincipled,
Europeanised dilettante, who is in love with her. It is late evening
and they are standing in the window of Antonia's house.

She did not answer. She seemed tired. They leaned side by side on the rail of the little balcony, very friendly, having exhausted politics, giving themselves up to the silent feeling of their nearness, in one of those profound pauses that fall upon the rhythm of passion. Towards the plaza end of the street the glowing coals in the brazeros of the market women cooking their evening meal gleamed red along the edge of the pavement. A man appeared without a sound in the light of a street lamp, showing the coloured inverted triangle of his bordered poncho, square on his shoulders, hanging to a point below his knees. From the harbour end of the Calle a horseman walked his soft-stepping mount, gleaming silver-grey abreast each lamp under the dark shape of the rider.

'Behold the illustrious Capataz de Cargadores,' said Decoud gently, 'coming in all his splendour after his work is done. . . .'[4]

There are several of the essentials here of Conrad's method. The personal relationship, intimately yet objectively suggested, is placed, by the immediate evocation of the whole plaza, securely within a larger social relationship, the private world related at once to the public world. The glowing coals, with their suggestion of after-passion, are at the same time surface-objective, adding to the visual reality of the scene, and atmospherically valuable, a kind of bridge between the two worlds. The market women and the man in his poncho are not merely picturesque (though they are that), they fill out involuntarily the social picture; they give a warmth and significance to the 'politics' that Antonia and Decoud (all too abstractly) have been discussing. And then, all within five sentences, the next character is on the scene: Nostromo, heralded by his conventional epithet 'illustrious'. And already the image most often associated with Nostromo has appeared, silver. Silver-grey is his horse in the moonlight, gleaming like the silver buttons which he has magnificently ripped off his tunic to give to his admirer Morenita, and like the treasure of the San Tome mine that will destroy him: all leading onward to the last sentence of the book when the name of Nostromo, the dead captive of the mine, has been cried out across the sea by his lover:

In that true cry of undying passion that seemed to ring aloud from Punta Mala to Azuera and away to the bright line of the horizon, over-hung by a big white cloud shining like a mass of solid silver, the genius of the magnificent Capataz de Cargadores dominated the dark gulf containing his conquests of treasure and love.[5]

Even more remarkable, however, than the technical achievement is the moral honesty and political insight which Conrad brings to his masterpiece.

'What is wanted here is law, good faith, order, security,' says Charles Gould, the owner of the silver mine. 'Anyone can declaim about these things, but I pin my faith to material interests. Only let the material interests once get a firm footing, and they are bound to impose the conditions on which alone they can continue to exist.'[6]

As against the mob the railway defended its property, but politically the railway was neutral.[7]

What a wealth of observation and understanding has gone to create such insights. The inadequacy of liberalism is most poignantly expressed in:

The feeling of pity for those men [the liberals], putting their trust into words of some sort, while murder and rapine stalked over the land. . . .[8]

And nearly all the liberals are shown as totally incapable of meeting the moment of danger.

A messenger from Hernandez, the notorious bandit, asks Charles Gould:

'Has not the master of the mine any message to send to Hernandez, the master of the Campo?'
The truth of the comparison struck Charles Gould heavily. In his determined purpose he held the mine, and the indomitable bandit held the Campo by the same precarious tenure. They were equals before the lawlessness of the land. It was impossible to disentangle one's activity from its debasing contacts. A close-meshed net of crime and corruption lay upon the whole country. . . .[9]

One tends to quote passages which show Conrad's consciously formulated understanding of the social situation he is recording; but the real test of a novel lies of course in its ability to convey artistically that understanding and for such a test the abstracted quotation is inadequate.

Mrs Gould's disillusionment with the effects of 'material interests' is almost complete when Dr Monygham says:

'There is no peace and no rest in the development of material interests. They have their law and their justice. But it is founded on expediency and is inhuman; it is without rectitude, without the continuity and the force that can be found only in a moral principle. Mrs Gould, the time approaches when all the Gould concession stands for shall weigh as heavily upon the people as the barbarism, cruelty and misrule of a few years back.'[10]

and at the close of the novel her husband must leave her, at a moment when she needs help and consolation, because there is labour unrest in the mine. The workers are disillusioned too. And Mrs Gould in her sad wisdom reflects:

It had come into her mind that for life to be large and full, it must contain the care of the past and of the future in every passing moment of the present.[11]

The tragedy of Nostromo is that he has none of this sense at all. He is without past and can have no future. He has no roots, he is an expatriate Italian. His great power and influence over the workers is exerted arbitrarily; he lives only for reputation. And when this is taken from him (by the failure of the liberal-capitalist alliance, which he has supported from no principle) he falls a prey immediately to the power and temptation of the silver of the mine. Thus Nostromo, though a 'natural' leader of the people and sharing their deepest hopes and aspirations as well as their fears and superstitions, Nostromo is useless as a leader because he is without principle. He is a careerist.

But if Nostromo does not understand the point of Mrs Gould's reflection, Conrad does; and it is in this profound comprehension that the greatness of the book ultimately lies. For it succeeds most wonderfully in capturing the truth of social movement. Engels once wrote:

'History makes itself in such a way that the final result always arises from conflicts between many individual wills, of which each again has been made what it is by a host of particular conditions of life. Thus there are innumerable intersecting forces, an infinite series of parallelograms of forces which give rise to one resultant—the historical event. This again may itself be viewed as the product of a power which, taken as a whole, works *unconsciously* and without volition. For what each individual wills is obstructed by everyone else, and what emerges is something that no one willed.[12]

It is extremely improbable that Conrad had ever read Engels; but this process which Engels describes in terms of science is precisely the total effect of *Nostromo*, achieved in terms of art—nothing less than the presentation (what George Eliot had aimed at in *Middlemarch*) of society in motion, history in the making.

Conrad succeeds moreover in the immensely difficult task of conveying the inter-relation between the individual and society, the one and the many. The people in *Nostromo* are what they are because they are part and parcel of a social situation; and at the same time they change and modify the situation. You cannot abstract them from the situation or the situation from them. When —like Decoud, the dandy, or Nostromo, the careerist—they do not accept their social obligations and attempt to live in isolation, lonely, haunted, without principle, nothing is left for them but death. Betrayal and isolation—that sense of guilt so powerful in the socially and intellectually dispossessed of our time—are powerful themes in all of Conrad's novels. In *Nostromo* the general stink of corruption (cf. Graham Greene), the grovelling fear of the terrified Hirsch (cf. Koestler), Nostromo's remorse at refusing the dying wish of his Italian foster-mother for a priest (cf. *Ulysses*), all bring something to this atmosphere, and the character of Dr Monygham who has under torture betrayed his friends (cf. Sartre) reinforces it. But the description of Monygham's release from jail after torture and imprisonment is well worth pausing on.

> He advanced one stick, then one maimed foot, then the other stick; the other foot followed only a very short distance along the ground, toilfully, as though it were almost too heavy to be moved at all; and yet his legs under the hanging angles appeared no thicker than the two sticks in his hands. A ceaseless trembling agitated his bent body, all his wasted limbs, his bony head, the conical, ragged crown of the sombrero, whose ample flat rim rested on his shoulders.
>
> In such conditions of manner and attire did Dr Monygham go forth to take possession of his liberty. And these conditions seemed to bind him indissolubly to the land of Costaguana like an awful procedure of naturalisation, involving him deep in the national life, far deeper than any amount of success or honour could have done. They did away with his Europeanism; for Dr Monygham had made himself an ideal conception of his disgrace. It was a conception eminently fit and proper for an officer and a gentleman. . . .[13]

Not merely is the sense of the social nature of man here extremely powerfully expressed, but there is also a subtle dissociation of the writer from the man he is describing. To permit himself the irony of the last sentence without jeopardising the compassion which

informs the whole description, Conrad needed all the artistic and
moral control which most of his successors have notably lacked.
The difference between the treatment of the dispossessed in
Nostromo and in the contemporary novels and plays of pessimistic
neurosis is that Conrad sees their problem not as a symbol of life
itself but only as a part of life. That he shares to a degree their despair is true and he expresses that despair most powerfully. Mrs
Gould in her disillusionment wonders for a moment whether
'there was something inherent in the nature of successful action
that carried with it the moral degradation of the idea'. But
though the theme is so poignantly done it retains the status of
a theme, over-topped by the prevailing vitality, the sense of life
developing.

Conrad succeeds in fact in the enormously difficult task (which
has defeated more 'politically-conscious' writers since) of revealing
imaginatively that 'every man is a piece of the continent, a part of
the main', and his triumph is the more remarkable because in his
personal outlook he would seem to have been far from clarity. This
is shown particularly in *Nostromo* in his inadequate attitude towards
'the mob' who never come to life as human beings. And it emerges
most significantly in a certain mistiness which, buried deep in the
language and symbolism of the book, does, we must admit, sometimes blur the stupendous realism of the achieved work of art. It is
not easy to isolate this quality—the quality that Mr Forster is
trying to catch when he writes of 'the central chasm of his tremen-
dous genius' and suggests that perhaps 'he is misty in the middle
as well as at the edges, that the secret casket of his genius contains
a vapour rather than a jewel'.[14] I do not find at the heart of *Nostromo*
anything like a vapour. On the contrary the quality of the imagery
in the greater part of the book is well compared to a jewel. Yet there
are moments in the novel when a sense of 'the cruel futility of
things' does seem to overcome Conrad—'the cruel futilty of lives
and deaths thrown away in the vain endeavour to attain an enduring
solution of the problem'.[15] With this sense—and it impregnates the
end of the novel: the enigmatic enquiry on Nostromo's face before
he dies, the presentation of his death as in some romantic sense a
triumph 'the greatest, the most enviable, the most sinister of all',
the ambiguity of the word 'dominated' in the final sentence—we
may associate, I think, the failure of Mrs Gould (and Conrad) ever
to define at all clearly the meaning of 'material interests'. This
recurring phrase plays so essential a part in the moral pattern of the
book that its precise significance cannot be ignored. This is the

climax of Mrs Gould's moral discovery in the novel, a discovery
from which Conrad never really dissociates himself:

> An immense desolation, the dread of her own continued life, descended
> upon the first lady of Sulaco. With a prophetic vision she saw herself
> surviving alone the degradation of her young ideal of life, of love, of
> work—all alone in the Treasure House of the World. The profound,
> blind suffering expression of a painful dream settled on her face with its
> closed eyes. In the indistinct voice of an unlucky sleeper, lying passive
> in the grip of merciless nightmare, she stammered out aimlessly the
> words:
> 'Material interest.'[16]

Objectively it is clear that 'material interest' stands for imperialism. It is the whole process and consequences of imperialist exploitation, so richly and concretely and humanely illuminated
throughout the length of the book, that Mrs Gould is brought up
against. Why should it matter then that Conrad does not use the
word (we are not after all reading sociology)? It matters, I think,
because it is the failure to recognise in its full theoretical and moral
significance the process of imperialism that leads to the element of
mistiness in *Nostromo*. Since 'material interest' is not given a
precise correlative (the correlative the whole novel cries out for) it
achieves a vague and uncontrolled one. The implication begins to
creep in (again Mrs Gould's remark about the degrading effect of
action is significant) that something in the very nature of things,
something beyond human control (yet never defined), is responsible
for the tragedy of *Nostromo*.

It is not of course the failure to use the word imperialism that
matters but a measure of failure to achieve artistic concreteness.
The reason for the failure is, I believe, fairly clearly explained in
Conrad's own experience. A Polish bourgeois nationalist, realistic
and unsentimental in his liberal sympathies and consequently forced
into exile, it was his attachment to Britain, his adopted country,
that seems to have clouded his objectivity. There is a significant
sentence in *Heart of Darkness* in which a distinction is drawn
between the British Empire and all other empires. Marlow, examining a map of the world, remarks (there is no artistic relevance to
the statement so that it can reasonably be abstracted): ' "There was
a vast amount of red—good to see at any time, because one knows
that some real work is done there." ' It was his loyalty to the
British Empire that prevented Conrad, despite the immense honesty
of his observation, from coming to an objective understanding of

imperialism as such, just as it was his position as a bourgeois nationalist that gave such poignancy to his presentation in *Nostromo* of Viola the Garibaldino, the austere and noble Italian democrat who fathers Nostromo. In this case, however, Conrad does achieve artistic objectivity, does succeed in mastering what must have been an almost overwhelming temptation to idealise (one recalls, too, the extraordinary discipline of objectivity which he brings to *Under Western Eyes*). For the Garibaldino, though personally admirable, is presented as ultimately ineffective. His pinciples are out of date; he cannot cope with the world of the San Tome silver mine. And he kills Nostromo whom his daughters love.

It is interesting that the two characters in *Nostromo* to the presentation of whom a residue of idealism clings (which is in fact responsible for the element of mistiness in the novel) are Mrs Gould and Nostromo himself—the woman and the worker. I believe it is not untrue to say that Conrad never fully came to terms with either. Dr Leavis has said (in his valuable pages on Conrad in *The Great Tradition*): 'About his attitude towards women there is perceptible, all the way through his literary career, something of the gallant, simple sailor.'[17] This seems to me completely true. Almost all Conrad's women are idealised and this idealisation is a subtle form of escape from reality. This is one aspect of the mistiness; the other lies in the 'enigmatic' quality of the masses. Once again the background of eastern Europe in the nineteenth century may be significant. There is much of Conrad himself in the dilemma of Razumov, the hero of *Under Western Eyes*:

> Between the two he was done for. Between the drunkenness of the peasant incapable of action and the dream-intoxication of the idealist incapable of perceiving the reason of things and the true character of men.[18]

The wonder is, indeed, not that there should be an unresolved element of haziness in *Nostromo* but that this great writer should have triumphantly achieved, against appalling odds, his 'moral discovery'—that vital sense of society changing, developing, becoming; of men mastering, with almost infinite difficulty, agony and error, the problems they have to master. There is always a danger that in 'explaining' with reference to his life and background a writer's qualities we degrade both the writer and ourselves. It is as an artist, not as a rather muddle-headed Polish *émigré*, that Conrad is of value to us. Nevertheless a passage from his description of his youth in *A Personal Record* is particularly illuminating:

An impartial view of humanity in all its degrees of splendour and misery together with a special regard for the rights of the unprivileged of this earth, not on any mystic ground but on the ground of simple fellowship and honourable reciprocity of services, was the dominant characteristic of the mental and moral atmosphere of the houses which sheltered my hazardous childhood: matters of calm and deep conviction both lasting and consistent, and removed as far as possible from that humanitarianism that seems to be merely a matter of crazy nerves or of a morbid conscience.[19]

We begin to see at such moments how it was that Conrad, standing on the very brink of the individualist quagmire of mysticism and neurosis, was yet able to draw back, to look with the deepest compassion and yet not permit himself to be drawn into the bog. Sometimes he seems almost overwhelmed by the difficulty of

appraising the exact shade of mere mortal man, with his many passions and his miserable ingenuity in error, always dazzled by the base glitter of mixed motives, everlastingly betrayed by a short-sighted wisdom.[20]

But he pulls back, always carefully dissociating himself from 'that humanitarianism that seems to be a matter of crazy nerves or of a morbid conscience', always avoiding the seductive hopelessness of Original Sin.

Conrad then has no conscious, intellectualised solution for the problems of the society which in *Nostromo* he depicts with so much truth and insight. And indeed it is foolish to talk glibly of the 'solution' offered by a work of art; the experience of the work of art is in itself a kind of solution, a synthesis, a discovery of the nature of the problem. But even on the level of immediate helpfulness this great novel holds its surprises. By a stroke of astonishing intuition the only man who is present with the dying Nostromo—symbol to Conrad of the People 'in his mingled love and scorn of life and in the bewildered conviction of being betrayed, of dying betrayed he hardly knows by what or by whom'[21] is none of the main characters of the novel whom we already know, but an obscure little workman, a 'small, frail, bloodthirsty hater of capitalists' who, personally unadmirable and presented ironically, yet speeds Nostromo to his death with the assurance that ' "The rich must be fought with their own weapons" '.[22]

3

MR BENNETT AND MRS WOOLF

Arnold Bennett, *The Old Wives' Tale* (1908)
H. G. Wells, *Tono-Bungay* (1909)
John Galsworthy, *The Man of Property* (1906)
Virginia Woolf, *To the Lighthouse* (1927)

It was in the 'twenties, those years of instability, uncertainty and experiment after the gigantic shock of the First World War, that Virginia Woolf wrote the famous essays in which, seeking a theoretical basis for her felt needs of creative experiment, she attacked the conventional novel of the day. It was true, of course, that even judged by their own standards and admirers, the novelists who were Mrs Woolf's principal targets had passed their prime. In her use of the word Edwardian with reference to Arnold Bennett and H. G. Wells and Galsworthy, there is a suspicion of malice which is in itself not quite fair. Today, that much further distant from the targets, we can perhaps more easily forgive the Edwardian novelists for being—whatever their other faults—Edwardian.

It will be the object of this chapter first to examine briefly the terms of Virginia Woolf's attack on the Edwardians, secondly to enquire whether, in the light of their own best work, the attack was justified, and finally to try to discover precisely what problems lay behind Mrs Woolf's discontent and whether she herself as a novelist succeeded in solving them.

The crux of Virginia Woolf's objections to the novels of Bennett, Wells and Galsworthy is that in their books, somehow or other, despite the formidable technical equipment, 'life escapes'.

Mr Wells, Mr Bennett and Mr Galsworthy have excited so many hopes and disappointed them so persistently that our gratitude largely takes the form of thanking them for having shown us what they might have done but have not done; what we certainly could not do, but as certainly, perhaps, do not wish to do. No single phrase will sum up the charge or grievance which we have to bring against a mass of work so large in its volume and embodying so many qualities, both admirable and the reverse. If we tried to formulate our meaning in one word we should say that these three writers are materialists. It is because they are concerned not with the spirit but with the body that they have disappointed us, and left us with the feeling that the sooner English fiction turns its back upon them, as politely as may be, and marches, if only into the desert, the better for its soul. Naturally, no single word reaches the centre of three separate targets. In the case of Mr Wells it falls notably wide of the mark. And yet even with him it indicates to our thinking the fatal alloy in his genius, the great clod of clay that has got itself mixed up with the purity of his inspiration. But Mr Bennett is perhaps the worst culprit of the three, inasmuch as he is by far the best workman. He can make a book so well constructed and solid in its craftsmanship that it is difficult for the most exacting of critics to see through what chink or crevice decay can creep in. There is not so much as a draught between the frames of the windows, or a crack in the boards. And yet—if life should refuse to live there?

And again:

If we fasten, then, one label on all these books, on which is one word materialists, we mean by it that they write of unimportant things; that they spend immense skill and immense industry making the trivial and the transitory appear the true and the enduring.

We have to admit that we are exacting, and, further, that we find it difficult to justify our discontent by explaining what it is that we exact. We frame our question differently at different times. But it reappears most persistently as we drop the finished novel on the crest of a sight—Is it worth while? What is the point of it all? Can it be that, owing to one of those little deviations which the human spirit seems to make from time to time, Mr Bennett has come down with his magnificent apparatus for catching life just an inch or two on the wrong side? Life escapes; and perhaps without life nothing else is worth while.[1]

It is perhaps worth emphasising, at this point, that Virginia Woolf was not, in the 'twenties, an isolated figure fighting a lone battle. The 'we' of her criticism is not the imperial pronoun of the Bloomsbury monarch. What she was saying, at any rate on its negative, critical side, would have been echoed by a dozen other serious novelists and critics and had indeed already been sketched, years before, by men like Hardy and James.

The recent school of novel-writers [Hardy wrote—and he was referring to Mrs Woolf's own targets] forget in their insistence on life, and nothing but life, in a plain slice, that a story must be worth the telling, that a good deal of life is not worth any such thing, and that they must not occupy the reader's time with what he can get at first hand anywhere about him.[2]

And Henry James, considering the novels of Arnold Bennett, had written in 1914:

When the author of *Clayhanger* has put down upon the table, in dense unconfused array, every fact required, every fact in any way invocable, to make the life of the *Five Towns* press upon us, and to make our sense of it, so full-fed, content us, we may very well go on for the time in the captive condition, the beguiled and bemused condition, the acknowledgement of which is in general our highest tribute to the temporary master of our sensibility. Nothing at such moments—or rather at the end of them, when the end begins to threaten—may be of a more curious strain than the dawning unrest that suggests to us fairly our first critical comment: 'Yes, yes—but is this *all*?' These are the circumstances of the interest—we see, we see; but where is the interest itself, where and what is its centre, and how are we to measure it in relation to *that*?'[3]

The complaint is essentially the same as Virginia Woolf's: 'Life escapes. . . .'

The attack is so broad, yet so fundamental, and its consequences in the later history of the novel have been so considerable that it will be worth while to look a little closer at some of the novels held up to criticism.

ARNOLD BENNETT

The Old Wives' Tale of Arnold Bennett is a spacious, leisurely novel which tells the story of the lives of two sisters born in the Potteries in the mid-nineteenth century. They are contrasted, Constance and Sophia, in a way not unlike Amelia Sedley and Becky Sharp, the one 'good', passive, exasperating, the other 'clever', active, courageous;* but it is typical of Arnold Bennett that Sophia Baines, for all her youthful ardour and high promise, should be unable to escape the background of Bursley and its values despite her initial act of rebellion. Sophia rebels against the drabness, the narrow philistinism, the joyless puritanism of the successful draper's shop in the Five Towns. She falls in love and runs off with her lover to Paris, to a world the opposite of the Five Towns in all its appearance and attraction. But the very nature of Sophia's elopement has been predetermined by the Five Towns. Her inexperience of life has prevented her from seeing till too late the true character of her lover, and though her Bursley hard-headedness enables her to look after herself, to force her lover to marry her and finally to salvage enough money to maintain herself when he leaves her, by this time the glory has gone out of her rebellion. Shrewdness, a protective independence and an eye for business have replaced ardour and generosity and love. So that, when she returns to Bursley to live out her last years with Constance, Sophia, for all her worldliness and experience, is seen to be as narrow, as incapable of true and generous happiness as her sister.

It is organised in four solid blocks of roughly equal length, this novel, the first dealing with the youth of the two girls at Bursley, the second and third with the respective stories of Constance and Sophia, the fourth with their reunion in late middle age and their deaths. Arnold Bennett, as is well known, was deeply influenced by the French naturalists of his day—Zola, the Goncourts and Maupassant; but in this novel at least their influence should not, I think, be overstressed. Zola's chief purpose, aesthetically speaking, was to achieve 'objectivity'; the naturalistic novel has, above all, the quality of the documentary. *The Old Wives' Tale*, on the other hand, for all its solidity, for all the fidelity of backcloth and detail in its setting, cannot adequately be described as a documentary. It has within it a more profound typicality, the kind of quality one associates rather with Dickens, which produces in the end a significant and moving pattern.

I am inclined to agree with Arnold Bennett's French critic M. Georges Lafourcade in seeing in *The Old Wives' Tale*, despite Bennett's own statement of his desire to make his novel an English

---

* If only the good could be clever
  And if only the clever were good
  This world would be nicer than ever
  We thought that it possibly could.

Miss Wordsworth's little verse might well be used as a text for a consideration of the main themes of nineteenth-century fiction.

Une Vie, the influence less of the later naturalists than of the older, more profound realism of Balzac. But what one may also say with confidence is that Bennett's interest in the French novel made him very conscious of the problems of form. 'An artist must be interested primarily in presentment, not in the thing presented,' he once wrote. 'He must have a passion for technique, a deep love of form.'[4] If *The Old Wives' Tale* has something of Dickens in it—betrayed perhaps by the tone and frequent facetiousness of the author's comment—there is also an austerity, a conscious concern over presentation, which is scarcely Dickensian.

The great problem of *The Old Wives' Tale* is why, fine and impressive novel as it is, it is not just that shade finer. It is almost a great novel—that is agreed—and yet, somehow, before the final affirmation of complete confidence one holds back. Why? E. M. Forster has tried his hand:

Time is the real hero of *The Old Wives' Tale*. . . . Our daily life in time is exactly this business of getting old which clogs the arteries of Sophia and Constance, and the story that is a story and sounded so healthy and stood no nonsense cannot sincerely lead to any conclusion but the grave. Of course we grow old. But a great book must rest on something more than an 'of course', and *The Old Wives' Tale* is strong, sincere, sad, it misses greatness.[5]

And Walter Allen, commenting on this very passage, has written:

It is not, it may be admitted, among the greatest novels. . . . It misses greatness if one believes there is that in man which transcends time. Then it must appear as a partial picture true only for 'our daily life in time'. But at the level of 'our daily life in time' *The Old Wives' Tale*, it seems to me, is in all essentials unassailable.[6]

The Old Wives' Tale seems to me to miss ultimate greatness because it presents a number of particular lives as Life and, in so doing, achieves the effect of 'reducing' life. As a picture of the life of Constance and Sophia Baines it is wonderfully successful. The Baines's shop, the relationships of the family, the development of the surrounding characters, are superbly done. We come to *feel* every stairway and passage, to relish every piece of furniture in that stuffy house on the corner of the Square in Bursley. As Henry James has, inimitably, put it: '. . . the canvas is covered, ever so closely and vividly covered, by the exhibition of innumerable small facts and aspects, at which we assist with the most comfortable sense of their essential truth.'[7] And Sophia's rebellion too we feel upon our pulses. We understand precisely her discontent and her vague but powerful aspirations; with ever-increasing admiration for Bennett's insight and honesty we watch her cope with her disillusionment and pay her subtle homage to the bourgeois virtues against which, insufficiently armed, she has once fought. We admire the remarkable lack of sentimentality with which Cyril Povey, Constance's 'artistic' son, is presented. One has only to compare him with George Eliot's Ladislaw or Galsworthy's Bosinney to grasp here the quality of Bennett's honesty. And finally we are moved, profoundly and bitterly, by Sophia's vision of her wasted life as she stands over the dead body of her worthless husband.

This much, then, of *The Old Wives' Tale* is wholly successful. What, bound up inextricably with it, limits our surrender is our sense that we are being asked here to contemplate the unrolling of Life itself. 'What Life Is' is the title of the fourth and final book of Bennett's novel and there is a pretension here which the novel for all its quality cannot fulfil. For to present the passage of time simply in terms of bitter, wasted aspiration, to claim for Sophia's tragedy a universal validity, is not good enough.

The Old Wives' Tale fails, in the end, to transmit a sense of the resilience of human experience, of the complexity of life's processes. It is, to return to Mr Allen's comment, precisely 'at the level of "our daily life in time"' that Arnold Bennett's novel is most assailable. For though it expresses, profoundly, Sophia's and Constance's daily life, it does not ultimately 'place' that life securely (or, rather, perilously, for life is not certain or stable) within time. Two examples will perhaps illuminate the point.

The historical development of the Five Towns, for instance, though much is made of it in the latter part of the book, is seen *only* from Constance's point of view. We see the changes in the Square, the movement from the old independent tradesmen to the new chain-store, from craft traditions to mass-production, the breakdown of the old civic spirit, the gradual encroaching from all sides of monopoly. All this is admirably caught. But because Bennett, for all his sympathy with the poor and the servants, conveys across to us nothing of the other side of the coin, the beginnings of trade union organisation for instance, the total effect of his picture of the Potteries is bound to lack something in vitality, is bound to give a certain sense of life's running down like a worn-out spring, which no doubt corresponds to Constance's own feelings but which is less than adequate as an expression of 'What Life Is'.

Similarly there is a weakness in the French section of the novel.

In one way this book is a very remarkable achievement. What Bennett succeeds in creating is a world, a way of life, emphatically not the Bursley way of life, so that when Sophia finally comes home and then looks back upon her life in Paris as she surveys the scene from Bursley Square, we have very effectively the sense of colour, brightness, a world of smart if brittle vivacity which throws into relief the grey and smoky provincialism of the Potteries. Parisian middle-class life is, in fact, contrasted with the middle-class life of North Staffordshire and the contrast is brilliantly effective. The weakness is that it is a limited contrast. Sophia's Paris remains essentially the tourist's Paris. This does not matter (it is from the point of view of Sophia herself quite credible) as far as Sophia's story is concerned. But for the larger claims of the novel it is inadequate. A great novelist who elected to deal with it would have seen for instance in the Paris Commune something that Arnold Bennett did not see.

These points bring us, I recognise, to the verge of a critical abyss. The type of criticism which complains that a writer did not write a book quite different from the one he set out to write has little value, no more has the sort of criticism that blames Jane Austen for leaving out the French Revolution. I am not suggesting that *The Old Wives' Tale* would necessarily have been a better novel if Bennett had included fuller descriptions of the Paris Commune or the rise of the Labour Movement in the Potteries. What I am suggesting is that a novelist must have a really rich imaginative understanding of anything that he writes about and that if his subject involves, as Arnold Bennett's did, a sense of broad social change and development, the novelist's own understanding of these issues is most relevant. He must convey somehow the sense of them even if it is outside the scope of his novel actually to describe them. One would not wish Sophia to understand what was happening in Paris in 1871—it is one of her characteristics that she could not; but Arnold Bennett should have understood and have conveyed across in some way that understanding. And if Bennett *had* understood or sensed something of the significance of the Paris Commune, then *The Old Wives' Tale* would have been artistically a better novel, for we should not then have had that uneasy sense of a false pretentiousness. The weakness of *The Old Wives' Tale* is that life itself is too closely identified with Sophia's and Constance's vision of life, so that when Sophia realises that her life has been wasted we are invited not simply to experience human pity and indignation but to say 'Ah, yes, Life's like that altogether'—which it isn't.

H. G. WELLS

H. G. Wells's *Tono-Bungay* is so totally different a novel from *The Old Wives' Tale* that it is perhaps hard to understand how any perceptive reader could ever have included the two authors in the same sentence. Wells, unlike Arnold Bennett, had little use for Turgenev, Flaubert and 'the Novel as an Art-Form' in the modern, Jamesian sense. His interest in fiction lay not in the production of the refined, 'aesthetic' sensation but in the stimulation of thought, the consideration of the vast sweep and movement of human activity.

'I warn you,' writes George Ponderevo, the hero and narrator of *Tono-Bungay*,

'. . . this book is going to be something of an agglomeration. I want to trace my social trajectory (and my uncle's) as the main line of my story, but as this is my first novel and almost certainly my last, I want to get in too all sorts of things that struck me, things that amused me and impressions I got—even though they don't minister directly to my narrative at all. I want to set out my own queer love experiences, too, such as they are, for they troubled and distressed and swayed me hugely, and they still seem to me to contain all sorts of irrational and debatable elements that I shall be the clearer-headed for getting on paper. And possibly I may even flow into descriptions of people who are really no more than people seen in transit, just because it amuses me to recall what they said and did to us, and more particularly how they behaved in the brief but splendid glare of Tono-Bungay and its still more glaring off-spring. It lit some of them up, I can assure you! Indeed, I want to get in all sorts of things. My ideas of a novel all through are comprehensive rather than austere. . . .'[8]

Wells undoubtedly thought of himself—in so far as he thought in such terms at all—as a novelist in the tradition of Fielding, Thackeray and Samuel Butler. The sort of ambition behind *Tono-Bungay* might indeed well be indicated by the famous phrase which Fielding used to describe *Joseph Andrews*, 'a comic epic poem in prose'.

Unfortunately the phrase reveals as well the fatal chink in Wells's armour. One cannot speak of *Tono-Bungay* as a poem in prose because it is in no satisfactory sense of the word a poem at all. Unlike *Joseph Andrews* or even *The Way of All Flesh*, it lacks that inner artistic unity, that unifying 'subject, one and indivisible' which creates patterns out of the apparently casual and wayward 'life' which is the raw material of Fielding's and Butler's novels.

There *ought* to be a pattern to *Tono-Bungay*. It is, so to speak, there for the asking. The rise and fall of Uncle Ponderevo might have been a poem in prose, so might have been the young manhood of George. There is, heaven knows, interest enough in the raw material of this book and comic observation enough and—rarest of all in modern novelists—an epic sense. Wells is a writer whom one tends to under-estimate until one actually returns to his books; then his vitality and his remarkable intelligence come as something of a surprise. It is an intelligence more rounded, more intimate, more inclusive than one had remembered. And this very phenomenon is significant. One does not carry from his books a vivid memory of Wells's many-sidedness because Wells himself achieved in his novels no adequate artistic expression of his own vision of life.

Part of the trouble would seem to be in his incurably slap-dash, slip-shod method of composition. He does not even give himself time to search for the right word, let alone organise his total material. Half the time he simply doesn't bother. For the chapter on 'How I stole the Quap' pseudo-Conrad will be good enough. It is not that he is incapable of good writing. As has been well said: 'His gift for vivid metaphor and the word used with a delight in its texture appears in welcome flashes amid oceans of turgid and shoddy thinking.'[9] He has indeed the real novelist's gift for making vivid the incidental scene, such as the pages which precede the death of Edward Ponderevo.

The stuffy little room was crowded when I reached it, and lit by three flickering candles. I felt I was back in the eighteenth century. There lay my poor uncle amidst indescribably tumbled bed-clothes, weary of life beyond measure, weary and rambling, and the little clergyman trying to hold his hand and his attention, and repeating over and over again:

'Mr Ponderevo, Mr Ponderevo, it is all right. It is all right. Only Believe! Believe on Me, and ye shall be saved!'

Close at hand was the doctor with one of those cruel and idiotic injection needles modern science puts in the hands of these half-educated young men, keeping my uncle flickeringly alive for no reason whatever. The *réligieuse* hovered sleepily in the background with an overdue and neglected dose. In addition the landlady had not only got up herself, but roused an aged crone of a mother and a partially imbecile husband, and there was also a fattish, stolid man in grey alpaca, with an air of importance—who he was and how he got there I don't know. I rather fancy the doctor explained him to me in French I did not understand. And they were all there, wearily nocturnal, hastily and carelessly dressed, intent upon the life that flickered and sank, making a public and curious show of its going, queer shapes of human beings lit by three uncertain candles, and every soul of them keenly and avidly resolved to be in at the death. The doctor stood, the others were all sitting on chairs the landlady had brought in and arranged for them.

And my uncle spoilt the climax, and did not die.

I replaced the little clergyman on the chair by the bedside and he hovered about the room.

'I think,' he whispered to me mysteriously, as he gave place to me, 'I believe—it is well with him.'[10]

And even here he cannot resist, in the sentence about hypodermic needles, dragging in his opinions about the medical profession. If only, one feels time and time again, he hadn't quite so many opinions, for they are always getting between the reader and the book, dissipating the effects he is achieving, rendering abstract whole scenes and stretches.

Tono-Bungay has a magnificent theme—the rise and fall of a business racketeer—a theme bristling with possibilities for the novelist as aware as Wells of the social ramifications of his subject. And he does make something of it; there is a passion behind *Tono-Bungay*, a passion of ideas which makes much 'good' modern writing seem paltry and insipid. From the opening tirades against aristocracy at Bladesover to the final defiant refusal to respect the 'paraphernalia of dignity' of the Parliament at Westminster issues are raised in this novel, notes touched which penetrate deep into the central human situations of our century. One can at least say of *Tono-Bungay* what one cannot say of a single widely-read novel of the last ten years or so, that here we have a humane, lively and morally alert intelligence directed upon some of the real, central public issues of the day.

But, this said, we are bound to ask why *Tono-Bungay* is not what it so patently ought to be—a great novel?

There are a number of directions from which one might approach the question. One might start, for instance, with Wells's failure to people adequately the world of his novel. There are almost no characters in *Tono-Bungay* who grip the imagination of the reader. Even Uncle Ponderevo himself is scarcely a person. He has, it is true, one or two characteristics, but they do not amount to a character. By the end of the book we know remarkably little about him—save that he is ebullient, feckless and means nobody any harm. And the same is true of the only two other characters who stick in the memory at all—Aunt Susan and George's wife Marion; we recognise them but we know almost nothing about them. And the remainder of the people in this novel we do not even recognise; they are not 'there' at all, George Ponderevo included.

Wells would probably have defended *Tono-Bungay* against such criticism on the grounds that he was not interested in the novel as a mere vehicle for the presentation of character. 'I would rather be called a journalist than an artist, that is the essence of it,' he wrote in a letter to Henry James. It is not 'personal relationships' (abstracted as they tended to be in the contemporary novel from their wider social setting) but something different, more 'scientific', that is his subject.

The novelist is going to be the most potent of artists, because he is going to present conduct, devise beautiful conduct, discuss conduct, analyse conduct, suggest conduct, illuminate it through and through. He will not teach, but discuss, point out, plead and display. We are going to appeal to the young and hopeful and the curious, against the established, the dignified and defensive. Before we have done we will have all life within the scope of the novel.[11]

Now this is all very well as an assertion of the potentialities of the novel, but to imagine that one can discuss conduct except in terms of actual human conflicts, or life except in terms of living creatures, is of course an illusion. It is one of the weaknesses of Wells, both as an artist and a thinker, that he tends to think of society as though it has some existence of its own outside of actual personal, social relationships. More specifically he tends to see everything in terms of his own consciousness and his own opinions, *from the outside*.

This is precisely the trouble with George Ponderevo in *Tono-Bungay*. He himself—the most essential character in the book— never really participates in any of the conflicts of the novel. He simply stands by, expressing opinions (which as often as not have no connection whatever with his actions) which do not change or develop in any significant way as a result of his experiences; indeed they cannot, for as a man, a living character, he experiences nothing. The only passage of personal relationship in the book that is at all convincing is the episode of his marriage with Marion, and even there no real human conflict is developed. The passages on Marion are given a certain vitality by the painful, masochistic quality of George's personal recollections (he is being more than usually honest with himself) not by the setting in motion of conflicting human forces.

Tono-Bungay as a novel is not conceived in terms of the real clashes, personal and social, involved in its magnificent theme, but entirely in terms of Wells's own consciousness as an observer and teacher. That it retains, as it does, so considerable a degree of vitality is, indeed, a tribute to the remarkable vivacity of Wells's intelligence, the passionate seriousness of what even Virginia Woolf rightly calls his genius. But as a work of art *Tono-Bungay* is inferior, for instance, to an American novel on a similar theme, F. Scott Fitzgerald's *The Great Gatsby*. Fitzgerald's novel is not without a strain of sentimentality, yet, because it reveals to us through the actual vibrant tensions of human relationships something of the actual, living horror of financial gangsterdom it *moves* us as *Tono-Bungay* fails to do.

Wells's novel seems to me to have a great deal in common with one of the most interesting and compelling of modern American films—Orson Welles's *Citizen Kane*, another story of a big-business tycoon. Both works, despite glaring inadequacies on the level of personal relationships, achieve, through a certain rather garish rhetoric—in the case of the film 'sound effects' and the crude, powerful results of exaggerated shadow in black-and-white photography—and an intuitive awareness of the broadest social implications of their subject, a fine effect of topical vitality, a lively illumination of certain highly significant themes of contemporary society. And at the same time both works have an underlying weakness of which the unsatisfactory personal insights are merely a symptom. In neither case is there any real struggle at the core of the drama. Kane, like Edward Ponderevo, flings himself hectically, powerfully, 'significantly' against—nothing.

George Ponderevo, summing up the significance of the career of Tono-Bungay, concludes: '. . . now it was open and manifest that I and my uncle were no more than specimens of a modern species of brigand, wasting the savings of the public out of a sheer wantonness of enterprise'.[12] It is a self-betraying sentence which, if one stops to analyse it, does not expose the truth about the Ponderevos of this world but shrouds it. 'Wasting the savings of the public.' How inadequate it is as an expression of what the Ponderevos have in terms of human exploitation and suffering actually done! And yet, almost inevitably, it follows from George's —and Wells's—own attitude to life. George Ponderevo, for all his mongrel-like defiance of the aristocracy of birth, is more than half a snob. He hates, it is true, the Bladesover régime which has humiliated him, but he never really escapes from the Bladesover values: the Honourable Beatrice Normandy will always remain his innermost ideal. More important still, George seems incapable of looking at the poor—the workmen who build Crest Hill, the sailors who man the *Maud Mary*, the dispossessed of Chatham and Gravesend—except with contempt as a species almost sub-human. Their chief characteristic is always that they are dirty. And in the last analysis it is this contempt of the working class which takes the artistic life out of *Tono-Bungay*, robbing it of a vital sense of human conflict, rendering it abstract when it should be art. The statement of opinion replaces the revelation of actual human and social tensions in *Tono-Bungay* because Wells runs away from these actual tensions and takes refuge in his *ideas* about them. As Caudwell insists in his brilliant if unsympathetic study[13] Wells is hamstrung by his petty-bourgeois outlook. If life escapes his clutches it is because he cannot bring himself or his main characters to participate fully and sympathetically in life as it actually is.

JOHN GALSWORTHY

The Man of Property, the first volume of *The Forsyte Saga*, became a 'best seller' and has, quite apart from its intrinsic qualities, a sociological interest on that account. For Galsworthy's novels were to become outstanding examples of 'middle-brow' literature, one of the most interesting literary phenomena of our time.

'Middle-brow' literature—not to beat about the bush—is inferior literature adapted to the special tastes and needs of the middle class and of those who consciously or not adopt the values of that class. It may be inferior for any number of reasons—every bad book has its own particular quality of badness—but to come within the category of 'middle-brow' it must maintain, whatever its particular brand of inferiority, certain proprieties sacred to the bulk of readers of the more superior lending-libraries. Though permitted to titillate with the mention and even the occasional vision of the unmentionable, it must never fundamentally shake, never stretch beyond breaking-point, certain secure complacencies. It is worth making this point because it would be quite wrong to see 'middle-brow' literature as merely qualitatively mediocre, better than bad literature but worse than good. Its distinctive feature is not its quality but its function.

It would not be fair to discuss *The Man of Property* simply as 'middle-brow'. As opposed to Galsworthy's later books, this novel has its core of seriousness, its spark of genuine insight which is not merely incidental but central to its very conception.

This spark is the theme of property and its effect upon the personal relationships of the Forsytes. *The Man of Property* begins as satire and it is, without reaching to any marked degree of subtlety, effective satire. What is particularly well conveyed is the significant contradiction in the relationships of the Forsyte clan between their dislike and suspicion of each other and their colossal sense of solidarity before any outside threat. The close, oppressive family ties based on no affection or even friendliness; the obligatory 'good living' in which no one shows the slightest talent or even much pleasure; the unceasing pressure and pre-occupation of acquisitiveness; the underlying assumption that human relationships are merely an extension of property relationships (a wife as a man's proudest possession): all this comes across effectively in the early chapters of the book. Robert Liddell has criticised Galsworthy's upholstery on the grounds that his method of presentation makes for merely crude differentiation between characters:

> Each Forsyte, or group of Forsytes, is built up from the background; we learn to know them apart by their furniture or their food. Old Jolyon had a study 'full of green velvet and heavily carved mahogany', and when he gives a family dinner the saddle of mutton, the Forsyte *pièce de résistance*, is from Dartmoor. Swithin has an 'elaborate group of statuary in Italian marble', which placed upon a lofty stand (also of marble), diffused an atmosphere of culture throughout the room! His mutton is Southdown. . . .
>
> This is not at all a clear way of distinguishing character. . . . If you collected and multiplied traits of the kind Galsworthy has here given, you might in the end arrive at some slight discrimination of character. But it is obvious that this is an extremely laborious way of doing things. One ought rather to deduce from the character of any Forsyte, if he had been well drawn, what sort of furniture he would be likely to have, and what he would be likely to offer one if one dined with him—if it is really a matter of interest to know.[14]

But surely this is to miss the whole point of Galsworthy's method. What *is* the character of any Forsyte abstracted from his furniture and his saddle of mutton? It is Galsworthy's strength, not his weakness, that he should so continuously insist in his presentation of the Forsytes on the crude material basis of their lives. It is nonsense to assume that behind Timothy or Swithin Forsyte there is some mysterious, disembodied 'character' waiting to be expressed by some sensitive artist like Virginia Woolf or Ivy Compton-Burnett.

Unfortunately the satire of *The Man of Property* is not sustained. It could not be, for there is insufficient sincerity, insufficient indignation behind it. The Forsyte characters, though credible enough, are too politely treated. Like all pusillanimous writers

Galsworthy is afraid to let his characters develop to their own logical extremes. He is for ever drawing back, blurring, sentimentalising. Of the 'pure' Forsytes only Soames is given anything of a free hand.

As it goes on *The Man of Property* becomes less and less satisfactory and this is because Galsworthy completely blurs the central conflict of the book—the conflict between humanity and property. The representatives of humanity—Irene, Bosinney, young Jolyon —turn out to be a poor lot; they are not more humane than the Forsytes, only more romantic. In the arguments between Soames and Bosinney over the house at Robin Hill, Soames is presumably meant to represent philistine materialism and Bosinney the artistic conscience, but in fact Soames's actions are, compared with Bosinney's, eminently justifiable. Bosinney's overspending in the face of numerous perfectly reasonable undertakings betrays not fine feelings but sheer incompetence; yet so hazy and wishy-washy and romantic are Galsworthy's positive values that we are invited to identify Bosinney and Irene with Art and Beauty, struggling against the tyranny of Property. In fact throughout *The Forsyte Saga* nobody really struggles against the tyranny of the Forsyte view of property. Young Jolyon, the humane rebel, is quite prepared (there isn't even a moment's conflict) to accept money from his father whose values and property-principles he affects to despise. Galsworthy's own positive is betrayed not as opposition to the Forsytes but as the sentimentalising of them. Old Jolyon is his ideal. That is why his satire which, as D. H. Lawrence remarked, had at the beginning 'a certain noble touch', soon fizzles out.

The satire, which in *The Man of Property* really had a certain noble touch, soon fizzles out, and we get that series of Galsworthian 'rebels' who are, like all the rest of the modern middle-class rebels, not in rebellion at all. They are merely social beings behaving in an anti-social manner. They worship their own class but they pretend to go one better and sneer at it. They are Forsyte *antis*, feeling snobbish about snobbery. Nevertheless, they want to attract attention and make money. That's why they are *anti*. It is the vicious circle of Forsytism. Money means more to them than it does to a Soames Forsyte, so they pretend to go one better, and despise it, but they will do anything to have it—things which Soames Forsyte would not have done.

If there is one thing more repulsive than the social being positive, it is the social being negative, the mere *anti*. In the great *débâcle* of decency this gentleman is the most indecent. In a subtle way Bosinney and Irene are more dishonest and more indecent than Soames and Winifred, but they are *anti*, so they are glorified. It is pretty sickening.[15]

Lawrence's essay, violent, passionate, cruel, is by far the finest criticism of Galsworthy.

The Man of Property has the elements of a very great novel, a very great satire. It sets out to reveal the social being in all his strength and inferiority. But the author has not the courage to carry it through. The greatness of the book rests in its new and sincere and amazingly profound satire. It is the ultimate satire on modern humanity, and done from the inside, with really consummate skill and sincere creative passion, something quite new. It seems to be a real effort to show up the social being in all his weirdness. And then it fizzles out.

Then, in the love affair of Irene and Bosinney, and in the sentimentalising of old Jolyon Forsyte, the thing is fatally blemished. Galsworthy had not quite enough of the superb courage of his satire. He faltered, and gave in to the Forsytes. It is a thousand pities. He might have been the surgeon the modern soul needs so badly, to cut away the proud flesh of our Forsytes from the living body of men who are fully alive. Instead, he put down the knife and laid on a soft, sentimental poultice, and helped to make the corruption worse. . . .

The Forsytes are all parasites, and Mr Galsworthy set out, in a really magnificent attempt, to let us see it. They are parasites upon the thought, the feelings, the whole body of life of really living individuals who have gone before them and who exist alongside with them. All they can do, having no individual life of their own, is out of fear to rake together property, and to feed upon the life that has been given by living men to mankind. . . .

Perhaps the overwhelming numerousness of the Forsytes frightened Mr Galsworthy from utterly damning them. Or perhaps it was something else, something more serious in him. Perhaps it was his utter failure to see what you were when you *weren't* a Forsyte. What was there *besides* Forsytes in all the wide human world? Mr Galsworthy looked, and found nothing. Strictly and truly, after his frightened search he had found nothing. But he came back with Irene and Bosinney and offered us that. Here! he seems to say, here is the anti-Forsyte! Here! Here you have it! Love! Pa-assion! PASSION.

We look at this love, this PASSION, and we see nothing but a doggish amorousness and a sort of anti-Forsytism. . . .[16]

It is true that Lawrence himself did not altogether escape the Forsytes. By identifying bourgeois society with society as such, by writing of 'social man' when he wanted to attack bourgeois man, he himself was paying a final, fantastic tribute to the Forsyte world. But nevertheless no one who has understood what Lawrence was driving at can ever return to Galsworthy quite seriously again. *The Man of Property* can be read today only as a museum-piece, not as a living work of art.

VIRGINIA WOOLF

'Life escapes. . . .' Because life, says Virginia Woolf, is not like this, not like what Bennett and Wells and Galsworthy present.

Look within and life, it seems, is very far from being 'like this'. Examine for a moment an ordinary mind on an ordinary day. The mind receives a myriad impressions—trivial, fantastic, evanescent, or engraved with the sharpness of steel. From all sides they come, an incessant shower of innumerable atoms; and as they fall, as they shape themselves into the life of Monday or Tuesday, the accent falls differently from of old; the moment of importance came not here but there; so that, if a writer were a free man and not a slave, if he could write what he chose, not what he must, if he could base his work upon his own feeling and not upon conviction, there would be no plot, no comedy, no tragedy, no love interest or catastrophe in the accepted style, and perhaps not a single button sewn on as the Bond Street tailors would have it. Life is not a series of gig-lamps symmetrically arranged; life is a luminous halo, a semi-transparent envelope surrounding us from the beginning of consciousness to the end. Is it not the task of the novelist to convey this varying, this unknown and uncircumscribed spirit, whatever aberration or complexity it may display, with as little mixture of the alien and external as possible? We are not pleading merely for courage and sincerity; we are suggesting that the proper stuff of fiction is a little other than custom would have us believe it.[17]

To the Lighthouse is an attempt by Virginia Woolf, her finest attempt perhaps, to write the alternative kind of novel.

It is extremely difficult to say with any sense at all of adequacy what *To the Lighthouse* is about. A good many critics have used the word 'symbolic', but there seems to be little agreement among them as to what is symbolic of what. I do not think it is a very helpful word to use in connection with Virginia Woolf's novel, though her own insistence, guarded from pretentiousness by a hundred not quite convincing modifications, on discussing the Meaning of Life[18] invites the term.

The trip to the lighthouse and the completion of Lily Briscoe's picture—the two principal binding themes of the book—do not 'stand for' something else. They are, rather, a framework, an essential part of the composition of the novel's total effect. *To the Lighthouse* is no more 'symbolic' than a picture by Cézanne and no more casual. In neither case can a mere paraphrase of the subject-matter convey anything of the essence of the artistic achievement. If one is asked 'What is that picture about?' one can only reply

'It is about itself; it is what the artist has painted; it is called Mont Ste Victoire or Still Life with Apples'. Similarly *To the Lighthouse* is itself. There is nothing to do with it except read it.

The mention of Cézanne is deliberate. In *Mr Bennett and Mrs Brown* there is a curious sentence which suggests that a sudden change took place in human character and perception in—the date is explicit—December 1910. Professor Isaacs has been, as far as I know, the first literary historian to suggest that this curious and apparently arbitrary date refers to the opening at the Grafton Galleries of the most famous of the post-Impressionist exhibitions.[19] Virginia Woolf was, of course, a member of a circle deeply, one might say passionately, involved in this event. Her friend Roger Fry and her brother-in-law Clive Bell were among the foremost publicists and defenders of modern French painting. And there can be little doubt that Virginia Woolf herself responded deeply both to the works of art involved and to the aims behind post-Impressionist painting.

> Into a world where the painter was expected to be either a photographer or an acrobat [wrote Clive Bell], burst the post-Impressionists, claiming that, above all things, he should be an artist.[20]

What Clive Bell is saying links up closely with Virginia Woolf's own discontents. Photographs and acrobats: 'materialists' absorbed in a barren technical dexterity. The complaint is essentially the same.

So too, to a high degree, is the answer. I am not qualified to offer an opinion as to whether Virginia Woolf's art derives the more from the Impressionist or the post-Impressionist painters.* Certainly impressionism (in the literary sense at least) seems to describe as well as any word her method, her concern with the texture of experience, her attempts to capture the 'myriad impressions' of the individual consciousness and to weld into a significant whole the apparently diverse and casual elements of a particular scene.

'Stream of consciousness', the term often applied to Mrs Woolf's technique, seems to me, as far as *To the Lighthouse* goes, to be scarcely more satisfactory than 'symbolism'. To Dorothy Richardson's novels, to parts of Proust's great book or to the final section of Joyce's *Ulysses*, the expression is appropriate. These writers do

---

* Professor Isaacs quotes suggestively (op. cit. p. 87) from R. A. M. Stevenson's book on Velasquez where such a phrase as 'the soft iridescence of the luminous envelope' occurs.

attempt, at least for a time, to portray reality wholly through the stream of impressions made on or through an individual's mind. But Virginia Woolf in this novel (*Mrs Dalloway* is a somewhat different case) has not the same object. Whose stream of consciousness could *To the Lighthouse* be said to convey? The focus point is constantly shifting. It is not through Mrs Ramsay's eyes that we view the whole, nor even through Lily Briscoe's, nor indeed through the eyes of any one character.

Virginia Woolf composes her novel very much as a painter—Lily Briscoe, for that matter—composes a picture. But of course there are differences. Time intrudes, for one thing. The 'Time Passes' section of the book seems to me its last successful passage, self-consciously arty and rather thin. But what is reminiscent of a painting is the overriding concern with texture and form. A touch is added here, a line extended there, a moment of apparently casual conversation posed against a break in the hedge, in order to achieve not story, not conflict, not character-insight, though all these elements may hover around, but the effect of the lived moment in time, the complex of colour and shape and shadow and tone of voice and prejudiced opinion and indigestion which is, Virginia Woolf insists, 'life'.

The subject of *To the Lighthouse*, if one may properly attempt to isolate it at all, is Mrs Ramsay and the effect of her presence, her very being, on the life around her. That effect cannot be fully understood or fully conveyed within her own lifetime, but in the final section, when she is already dead, she is still the main figure. It is she who leads Lily Briscoe to the sense of momentary completeness, the moment of vision which is the climax of the book; and Mrs Ramsay's presence is indeed an essential part of that vision. (In the first section she is merely a 'triangular purple shape' in Lily's picture.) The journey to the lighthouse, James's flash of triumph, is the completion too of the first moment of the book, the triangular relationship between Mr and Mrs Ramsay and James revealed in the opening pages of the novel.

In what sense may life be said, in *To the Lighthouse*, not to escape? In the sense, perhaps, that there is nothing second-hand about this novel, that the convention in which it is written permits Virginia Woolf to convey with extraordinary precision a certain intimate quality of felt life. The dinner scene which is at the centre of the novel is a piece of writing worth comparing with, say, Galsworthy's description of dinner at Swithin Forsyte's in the early part of *The Man of Property*. Galsworthy's dinner is well described; we get a sense of what kind of room Swithin's dining-room is, of what each of the characters sitting round the table is like, of the social interplay going on throughout the meal and the quality of the saddle of mutton. But the effect is, compared with Virginia Woolf's, a surface effect. We are not made aware of the moment-by-moment texture of feeling, the intricate pattern of reaction, the wispish, wayward flitting of consciousness, the queer changes in tempo of the responses, the *taste* of the food, the sudden violent swoops of emotion and the strange, enhanced significance of outside, inanimate, casual things, a shadow on the table, the pattern of the cloth.

In the description (if it is not too intractable a word) of the dinner in *To the Lighthouse* a dimension is introduced which in Galsworthy's writing is altogether absent. And that dimension— let us call it the impression of the momentary texture of experience— has the effect which Virginia Woolf was seeking when she used the words 'luminous halo' to describe life. There is a luminous quality in the general effect of *To the Lighthouse* which is what gives the novel its particular value. These people may not be very interesting, neither their activities nor their mental pre-occupations may concern us very much when we abstract and think about them; but they are alive. They breathe the air, they catch the fragrance of the flowers or the tang of the sea, they eat real food, they *know* one another. Whatever they are they are not cardboard figures or puppets or caricatures (we have come to the furthest point from the comedy of humours); and because they are in this physical—one might almost say primitive—sense alive they have a kind of resilience which is rare in literature. Robert Liddell has said well: 'The truth is perhaps this: while we know the characters of Miss Austen as we know our friends (if we are abnormally observant), we know Mrs Woolf's characters as we know ourselves.'[21] This is a reference of course to the quality and not the quantity of knowledge involved. The effect of *To the Lighthouse* is the absolute antithesis of flatness.

And yet . . . ? Having said this, having relished what is in this novel unique and exquisite, have we not missed out what is most important of all? Is it right to resist the temptation, after one has finished *To the Lighthouse* and remained for a while sensitive to its spell, to slam it with as vulgar a gesture as one can muster and permit to fall the brutal words: 'So what?'

The trouble with *To the Lighthouse*, it seems to me, is the quite simple and quite fundamental trouble that it is, when all is said, not about anything very interesting or important. That, of course, is putting it too simply and leaving oneself wide open to some obvious rejoinders. In one sense all life is, from the writer's point of view, equally important and when a novelist achieves an effect of expression which we feel to be 'good' that is that. The effect of *To the Lighthouse* is something new in literature (and we cannot say that of the novels of Bennett or Galsworthy); in the moments of enjoyment of the book we experience something we have not experienced before and our sensibility is, by that experience, refined. In this sense Virginia Woolf may justly be regarded as a finer, more truly artistic writer than any of the Edwardian novelists we have discussed. But that is not the only thing to be said.

D. S. Savage, in an essay on Virginia Woolf, has written:

> The distinguishing feature of Virginia Woolf's apprehension of life lies . . . in its passivity; and furthermore, she subscribed unwittingly . . . to a view of life which placed a primary emphasis upon the object. One recalls the passive function ascribed to the mind ('The mind *receives* a myriad impressions') and the atomistic conception of experience ('From all sides they come, an incessant *shower of atoms*') revealed in the essay 'Modern Fiction'. . . . Virginia Woolf's search for 'significance' on the primitive level of primary sensational perceptions . . . was chimerical from the beginning. And, indeed, it is a typical feature of the characters of her novels to be altogether lacking in the capacity for discriminating within experience. They are passively caught up in the streams of events, of 'Life', of their own random perceptions.[22]

I think Mr Savage underrates Virginia Woolf's powers but he seems to me to make here an essential point. Upon what is this subtle apparatus of sensibility after all exercised? Upon what vision of the world, what scale of human values, is it based? What is lacking in *To the Lighthouse* is a basic conflict, a framework of human effort. What does Lily Briscoe's vision really amount to? In what sense is the episode in the boat between James and Mr Ramsay really a culmination of their earlier relationship?

Are they really the alternative possibilities, *The Old Wives' Tale* and *Tono-Bungay* and *The Man of Property* on the one hand, *To the Lighthouse* on the other? What are we to make, looking back at it now after a quarter of a century, of Virginia Woolf's thesis?

In the first place we must insist, I think, that in lumping together Arnold Bennett, Wells and Galsworthy, Virginia Woolf and her allies were, from the point of view of literary criticism, making a tactical mistake, for the three novelists are fundamentally, not merely superficially, very different in method and in value.

They do, of course, in contrast with Virginia Woolf herself, have something in common. Not only does each of the three Edwardian novels we have discussed have a plot in the sense that *To the Lighthouse* can scarcely be said to have one (though the plot of *Tono-Bungay* is in all conscience flimsy enough); more important, they share the assumption, denied by Mrs Woolf, that a 'sense of life' can be conveyed by objective description of other people and scenes as opposed to the subjective impressions of a number of individual consciousnesses. And Bennett and Wells and Galsworthy are indeed, as Virginia Woolf accuses them, 'materialists' in the sense that they see their characters and stories as emerging out of, and indeed inseparable from, a particular material situation.*

I think it is possible that in the attacks of Virginia Woolf and Hardy and James on the Edwardians two separate issues get muddled up. On the one hand is the feeling that 'they write of unimportant things', that there is something essential missing in these novels which makes them less than wholly satisfying; on the other is the conviction that this missing something, this ultimate failure in greatness, is intricately connected with the upholstery of their novels, their emphasis on material detail, their naturalistic method.

If we look back on *The Old Wives' Tale* and *Tono-Bungay* and *The Man of Property* (remembering that each shows the author at his very best, does him perhaps rather more than justice) we will agree, I think, with the general complaint that there is indeed something wrong with these novels, even with *The Old Wives' Tale* which is the best of them. But if we begin to ask just *what* is wrong then the answer quickly becomes not merely more complex than Virginia Woolf indicates but also rather different in general direction.

There is, of course, something in Virginia Woolf's attack on the methods of 'naturalism'. When, in *Mr Bennett and Mrs Brown*, she asked the Edwardian novelist how she should set about describing Mrs Brown, the woman she meets in the train, they replied.

'Begin by saying that her father kept a shop in Harrogate. Ascertain

* One does not wish to become involved in philosophical distinctions but it is worth insisting that Mrs Woolf was of all writers the least justified in using the word 'materialist' as a term of abuse. For her own method, based on her view of consciousness as an 'incessant shower of innumerable atoms' is in fact an expression of pure, crude, mechanical Lockean materialism.

the rent. Ascertain the wages of shop assistants in the year 1878. Discover what her mother died of. Describe cancer. Describe calico. Describe——' [23]

It is worth comparing this with an actual statement by Zola about the aims of the naturalist writer:

A naturalist writer wants to write a novel about the stage. Starting from this point without characters or data, his first concern will be to collect material, to find out what he can about this world he wishes to describe. He may have known a few actors and seen a few performances. . . . Then he will talk to the people best informed on the subject, will collect statements, anecdotes, portraits. But this is not all. He will also read the written documents available. Finally he will visit the locations, spend a few days in a theatre in order to acquaint himself with the smallest details, pass an evening in an actress's dressing-room and absorb the atmosphere as much as possible. When all this material has been gathered, the novel will take shape of its own accord. All the novelist has to do is to group the facts in a logical sequence. . . . Interest will no longer be focussed on the peculiarities of the story—on the contrary, the more general and commonplace the story is, the more typical it will be. . . .[24]

Clearly Mrs Woolf was not merely tilting at windmills.

But the question arises as to whether it is in fact their 'material-ism' in Virginia Woolf's meaning that limits the achievements of the writers of the 'naturalistic' order. I do not think it is. What is ultimately unsatisfactory about Zola as a novelist—and the same applies at least in some measure to such English novels as George Gissing's *In the Year of Jubilee*, George Moore's *Esther Waters* and Somerset Maugham's *Of Human Bondage* as well as to *The Old Wives' Tale*—is a failure to distinguish between surface verisimili-tude and underlying typicality. These novels are all 'true to life' in the sense of being honest descriptions of what can and does actually happen in life, and yet they give us, in varying degrees, a feeling that 'life escapes' because human life is at once more resilient, less 'flat', has—so to speak—more possibilities than these books suggest.

Professor Lukàcs has made a suggestive contribution to the question by his comparison of two kinds of 'typicality'—that naturalism which concentrates on the typical in the sense of the average, the ordinary, the essentially casual, and that deeper realism which gets hold of the extreme possibilities inherent in a situation and gains a more profound typicality through a concentration on the truly significant tensions within that particular chunk of 'life'.*

* Lukàcs says of Zola and the naturalists: 'A mechanical average takes the place of the dialectic unity of type and individual; description and analysis is substituted

A large number of honest and worthy late Victorian and Edwardian novels are naturalistic in Lukàcs's limiting sense and their
limitation is linked, I think, with a deep social pessimism. Life in
Britain at the turn of the century seems to the writers depressing
and frustrating and yet, because they can be confident of no alternative possibilities, life is like this, like the final section of *The Old
Wives' Tale*. Either they discover no significant pattern at all or
else they give to a situation which may be 'true' but is not, in the
deepest sense, typical (or, if one prefers the word, symbolic) a
significance which it will not bear and which therefore has a limiting, constricting effect on the total impression of their work.

It is her apprehension of at least something of this problem
which seems to me to give what force it has to Virginia Woolf's
attack on the Edwardians. The weakness of her criticism lies in her
unsatisfactory diagnosis of the causes of her discontent and is
further expressed in the limitations of her own positive answer.
The social realists of the turn of the century (and it is only by
stretching the point perhaps illegitimately that one can include
Wells among them at all*) are all vulnerable to criticism. Even the
best of them—the Bennett of *The Old Wives' Tale*, the Gissing of
The Odd Women, Arthur Morrison in *The Hole in the Wall*—seem
somehow overpowered by their material and veer either towards
flatness or towards a rather bogus forced quality which can perhaps
best be described as neo-Dickensian. None of them succeeded to
the extent, for instance, Gorky did in Russia in meeting the challenge
of a social situation which demanded from its realist artists not
merely subjective honesty but a radical re-examination of the very
basis of their sensibility.

And yet, whatever is the matter with these novels, it is certainly
not their firm connection with material reality. On the contrary, it
is this very quality that gives to *The Old Wives' Tale*, when all is
said and balanced, so much more 'life' than *To the Lighthouse*. 'Life

for epic situations and epic plots. . . . Average characters whose individual traits are
accidents from the artistic point of view . . . act without a pattern, either merely side
by side or else in completely chaotic fashion.'[25] And of Tolstoy: 'The hallmark of
the great realist masterpiece is precisely that its intensive totality of *essential* social
factors does not require, does not even tolerate, a meticulously accurate or pedantic-
ally encyclopaedic inclusion of all the threads making up the social tangle; in such a
masterpiece (as *Anna Karenina*) the most essential social factors can find total expression in the apparently accidental conjunction of a few human destinies.'[26]

* The 'social realist' side of Wells is, of course, mixed up with his propagandist
intention and links him with those interesting Victorian propagandist novels,
Kingsley's *Alton Locke* and Mark Rutherford's *The Revolution in Tanner's Lane*,
books deeply moving in the earnest humanity of their authors' vision but scarcely
satisfying as novels.

escapes. . . .' But has not more life indeed escaped from Bennett's novel than ever gets into Virginia Woolf's? Bennett has let something essential slip through his fingers; but what remains imposes itself on the imagination, illuminates the broad span of human experience, with an overall vitality which Virginia Woolf for all her insistent questionings about the purpose of Life and her subtle evocation of the texture of the lived moment cannot be said to achieve.

There is again more 'life', though no doubt less 'sensibility' of the accepted, middle-class sort, even in a rather tedious flat novel like *Esther Waters* than in the work of Dorothy Richardson, in which the implications of Virginia Woolf's theory of life as 'an incessant shower of innumerable atoms' are consistently accepted. The truth is that though the late Victorian and Edwardian social realists were, so to speak, realists *manqués*, writers who could not see the wood for the trees and therefore tended always to 'reduce' life, they were at least working in a tradition that had some basic validity, some possibility of expansion and development, whereas the alternative direction of Virginia Woolf, the development of a cult of sensibility, inadequately based on the realities of the social situation, was likely to lead nowhere very useful at all.

What is positive in Virginia Woolf's achievement is her expression of discontent with the dreary flatness of so much naturalistic writing and her reassertion of the luminousness of life, her sense of the value and dignity and creativeness of apparently casual experience. She writes of James Ramsay in the opening section of *To the Lighthouse*:

> Since he belonged, even at the age of six, to that great clan which cannot keep this feeling separate from that, but must let future prospects, with their joys and sorrows, cloud what is actually at hand, since to such people even in earliest childhood any turn of the wheel of sensation has the power to crystallise and transfix the moment upon which its gloom or radiance rests, James Ramsay, sitting on the floor cutting out pictures from the illustrated catalogue of the Army and Navy Stores, endowed the picture of a refrigerator as his mother spoke with heavenly bliss. It was fringed with joy.[27]

In the method which such a passage illustrates may be seen the direction of the emphasis Virginia Woolf brought to the novel. That refrigerator fringed with joy had had no place in the naturalistic tradition; a radiance, which in one sense is life itself, comes back. Yet its reintroduction into the picture may have been bought, it now must seem, at too dear a price.

4

D. H. LAWRENCE: THE RAINBOW

(1915)

I have chosen *The Rainbow* among the novels of D. H. Lawrence not because I am sure it is Lawrence's best book but because it has so much, so many aspects, of the essential Lawrence in it. And yet I want it to be clear right away that I am not using *The Rainbow* to illustrate Lawrence's ideas.

With Lawrence it is particularly difficult to talk about the novels rather than the ideas. Certainly one cannot discuss the novels *without* the ideas, but that is a different proposition. My point is that the novels, though they express—as any work of art must— their author's philosophy, are greater than that philosophy once it is abstracted or expressed in any other terms than the novels themselves.

It is part of Lawrence's greatness as an artist that he had no use for art for art's sake—in the way the phrase is generally understood. 'The novel can help us to live, as nothing else can,' he declares in his essay 'Morality and the Novel'.[1] He is out to help us to live. But he adds to his sentence: '. . . as nothing else can, no didactic scripture anyhow. . . .' The artist-prophet is not a preacher. But neither is he a take-it-or-leave-it mere presenter of things as they seem to be.

I can only write what I feel pretty strongly about, and that, at present, is the relation between men and women. After all, it is the problem of today, the establishment of a new relation, or the readjustment of the old one, between men and women.[2]

This sense that things as they are are a 'problem', not merely an occurrence, and that writing about them implies changing them is extremely strong in Lawrence and important.

That is one of the reasons why the temptingly simple view of Lawrence's work—that he starts well in *The White Peacock* and *Sons and Lovers* as a great realist artist and declines in value as his philosophy gets the upper hand—is not quite good enough, even as a simplified generalisation. It is true that Lawrence, after *Sons and Lovers*, might have taken a different path and that never again, even in the best parts of *The Rainbow* or *Women in Love* or *Lady Chatterley's Lover*, did he write anything so magnificent as, at any rate, the first half of that book; but that is not the whole story.

The sentence preceding the one I have already quoted from 'Morality and the Novel' runs:

The novel is a perfect medium for revealing to us the changing rainbow of our living relationships.[3]

It is a very significant sentence, both as an indication of the scope and splendour of Lawrence's intention and as a pointer to the meaning of the central symbol of *The Rainbow*. In a later—and generally under-estimated—novel, *Kangaroo*, we find another sentence worth attention:

The rainbow was always a symbol to him—a good symbol: of this peace. A pledge of unbroken faith, between the universe and the innermost.[4]

This is what *The Rainbow* is about, the living relationships of men and women, the struggle to achieve peace and fulfilment one with another within the colossal compass of the ranged arch of the visible universe. We are reminded perhaps of the imagery Shakespeare creates in *Antony and Cleopatra*, the play in which above all others he grapples with this problem of the relation of the personal to the public life, the innermost and the universe. His images are less mystical than Lawrence's. It is the arch of the ranged Roman Empire that spans the world, and when Cleopatra gives us her final superb vision of Antony whose 'rear'd arm crested the world' we recognise in her words a thread of imaginative self-deception which merits in all its ambiguity the word romantic. But the central image of the arch, which at once rears upwards and yet contains, is the connecting element I would wish, without overstressing the analogy, to indicate.

The rainbow is the pledge of rightness, of continuity (it has therefore a direct sexual connotation) and adjustment. Its appearance at the end of the novel involves the evocation of many of the underlying fertility images of our culture, including the whole idea of the delivery of the waste land from the curse of sterility. But before that final image is projected Lawrence has continuously worked on our imagination so that the rainbow, though it retains (as we shall see) an unsatisfactory element of mysticism, has behind it a great deal of profoundly significant concrete experience.

The novel is the revelation of a series of personal relationships: primarily those of Tom Brangwen and Lydia Lensky, Will and Anna, Ursula and Skrebensky. Lawrence knows prefectly well that no personal relationship exists in a vacuum. None of the characters in *The Rainbow* is abstracted from the situations and relationships and experiences that has made him what he is. The characters change, develop, yet remain unified. Anna the complacent, easygoing, rather repulsive mother of a drawn-out family of nine children is still the same person as the wild, self-possessed yet frightened little girl who first comes to the Marsh with her foreign mother. Lawrence, for all his apparent tendency to generalise about personal relationships, is always aware of the disparate factors which go to make up every situation. He may have written to Edward Garnett about *The Rainbow* in a letter which has perhaps been over-quoted:

> . . . You mustn't look in my novel for the old stable ego of character. There is another ego, according to whose action the individual is unrecognisable, and passes through, as it were, allotropic states which it needs a deeper sense than any we've been used to exercise to discover—states of the same single radically unchanged element.[5]

But the fact remains that the characters in *The Rainbow* are, even in the conventional sense of novel personages, individual characters, that is to say, clearly recognisable from one another, unique beings whose uniqueness we may come to know through unfamiliar means but who, once apprehended, are quite describable in alternative and more conventional terms.

The means by which the nature of the personal relationships is conveyed across to the reader constitutes of course the principal originality of Lawrence as a novelist. It is insufficient to speak of it as a technical originality because the technical method is the expression of the originality in Lawrence's vision. Because he saw differently from other novelists he had to write differently.

The early chapters of *The Rainbow* are technically comparatively straightforward. Occasionally, at moments of climax, one comes upon such a sentence as 'Then he burst into flame for her, and lost himself'. But the reader is likely to take such a moment pretty much in his stride without being aware that he is involved in any very unusual way of writing. It is with the remarkable chapter 'Anna Victrix' that it becomes clear that Lawrence is using words not in a slightly eccentric but in a radically unusual way. It is here that the remarks about character in the letter to Edward Garnett become relevant, for it is patent that the description of the first year or so of Anna's marriage cannot be read as normal naturalistic descriptive writing.

Walter Allen has discussed the question in his essay, 'D. H. Lawrence in Perspective':

What interests him in his characters, is not the social man, the differentiated individual, but the seven-eighths of the iceberg of personality that is submerged and never seen, the unconscious mind, to which he preaches something like passivity on the part of the conscious. This accounts for the difficulty so many people find when first reading Lawrence. His convention has to be accepted, just as the conventions of any artist must be, if you are to read him with pleasure and profit. It accounts, too, for so many mannerisms of style that are usually considered blemishes: a Lawrence character 'dies', 'swoons', is 'fused into a hard bead', 'lacerated', 'made perfect', time and time again. He is, if you like, fumbling for words, words with which to describe the strictly indescribable. Yet the language he uses is true to the rhythm of the life of the unconscious.[6]

It is perhaps permissible to doubt whether Mr Allen—or anyone else—knows what constitutes the rhythm of the life of the really unconscious. But he makes an important point in his insistence that Lawrence's convention has to be accepted if we are to read him at all. And what is impressive about this curious, intense convention through which the emotional relationship of Will and Anna Brangwen is conveyed, is that it does very remarkably achieve a sense of the conflict and interplay of human personalities. 'Anna Victrix' is the description of a year of marriage, of the meeting, joining, breaking and adaptation of two human beings. It is not naturalistic save in the odd detail, the sudden imposed scene, which sets and places the relationship, holds it to earth, makes it concrete and not abstract. Most of the time the effect is achieved by repetition (in no other way could he so successfully compass time, trivialities, boredom), by rhythm, and by insistent symbolic-seeming words like dark, burning, obliteration, destroyed, etc., and by images of flowers and every kind of fertility symbol.

I do not think we need to accept Lawrence's theories about the unconscious or the fashionable tarradiddle about 'the seven-eighths of the iceberg of personality that is submerged and never seen' to recognise either the power or the justice of the art in 'Anna Victrix'. That emotional relationships of the more intense kind are likely to be more fully and deeply conveyed in writing which encompasses and exploits rhythms and images which are scarcely conceivable in the colder terms of a fully rationalised prose is not a proposition which necessarily involves a capitulation to mystical obscurantism.

Lawrence sees human relationships essentially in terms of a conflict out of which a synthesis is possible but by no means inevitable. It is his ability to convey across this sense of conflict—which does indeed go deeper than a rational level—which gives his finest descriptions of personal relationships their unique force and insight.

In each of the relationships which Lawrence examines the image of the arch which is to find its final expression as the rainbow is involved. The most complete and satisfactory of the relationships is that achieved by Tom Brangwen and his Polish wife, Lydia. It is not an easily achieved happiness. There is a foreignness between them, he the working farmer, she the half-aristocratic, rather intelectual Polish lady; there is the problem of the little Anna, the step-child; there is the inadequacy in his whole conception of a marriage-relationship, the sort of inadequacy wonderfully conveyed in this passage:

The evening came on, he played with Anna, and then sat alone with his own wife. She was sewing. He sat very still, smoking, perturbed. He was aware of his wife's quiet figure, and quiet dark head bent over her needle. It was too quiet for him. It was too peaceful. He wanted to smash the walls down, and let the night in, so that his wife should not be so secure and quiet, sitting there. He wished the air were not so close and narrow. His wife was obliterated from him, she was in her own world, quiet, secure, unnoticed, unnoticing. He was shut down by her.

He rose to go out. He could not sit still any longer. He must get out of this oppressive, shut-down, woman-haunt.

His wife lifted her head and looked at him.

'Are you going out?' she asked.

He looked down and met her eyes. They were darker than darkness, and gave deeper space. He felt himself retreating before her, defensive, whilst her eyes followed and tracked him down.

'I was just going up to Cossethay,' he said.

She remained watching him.

'Why do you go?' she said.

His heart beat fast, and he sat down, slowly.

'No reason particular,' he said, beginning to fill his pipe again, mechanically.

'Why do you go away so often?' she said.

'But you don't want me,' he replied.

She was silent for a while.

'You do not want to be with me any more,' she said.

It startled him. How did she know this truth? He thought it was his secret.

'Yi,' he said

'You want to find something else,' she said.

He did not answer. 'Did he?' he asked himself.

'You should not want so much attention,' she said. 'You are not a baby.'

'I'm not grumbling,' he said. Yet he knew he was.

'You think you have not enough,' she said.

'How enough?'

'You think you have not enough in me. But how do you know me? What do you do to make me love you?'

He was flabbergasted.

'I never said I hadn't enough in you,' he replied. 'I didn't know you wanted making to love me. What do you want?'

'You don't make it good between us any more, you are not interested. You do not make me want you.'

'And you don't make me want *you*, do you now?' There was a silence. They were such strangers.

'Would you like to have another woman?' she asked.

His eyes grew round, he did not know where he was. How could she, his own wife, say such a thing? But she sat there, small and foreign and separate. It dawned upon him she did not consider herself his wife, except in so far as they agreed. She did not feel she had married him. At any rate, she was willing to allow he might want another woman. A gap, a space opened before him.

'No,' he said slowly. 'What other woman should I want?'

'Like your brother,' she said.

He was silent for some time, ashamed also.

'What of her,' he said. 'I didn't like the woman.'

'Yes, you liked her,' she answered persistently.

He stared in wonder at his own wife as she told him his own heart so callously. And he was indignant. What right had she to sit there telling him these things? She was his wife, what right had she to speak to him like this, as if she were a stranger.

'I didn't,' he said. 'I want no woman.'

'You, you would like to be like Alfred.'

His silence was one of angry frustration. He was astonished. He had told her of his visit to Wirksworth, but briefly, without interest, he thought.

As she sat with her strange dark face turned towards him, her eyes watched him, inscrutable, casting him up. He began to oppose her. She was again the active unknown facing him. Must he admit her? He resisted involuntarily.

'Why should you want to find a woman who is more to you than me?' she said.

The turbulence raged in his breast.

'I don't,' he said.

'Why do you?' she repeated. 'Why do you want to deny me?'

Suddenly, in a flash, he saw she might be lonely, isolated, unsure. She had seemed to him the utterly certain, satisfied, absolute, excluding him. Could she need anything?

'Why aren't you satisfied with me?—I'm not satisfied with you. Paul used to come to me and take me like a man does. You only leave me alone or take me like your cattle, quickly, to forget me again—so that you can forget me again.'

'What am I to remember about you?' said Brangwen.

'I want you to know there is somebody there besides yourself.'

'Well, don't I know it?'

'You come to me as if it was for nothing, as if I was nothing there. When Paul came to me, I *was* something to him—a woman, I was. To you I am nothing—it is like cattle—or nothing——'

'You make me feel as if *I* was nothing,' he said.

They were silent. She sat watching him. He could not move, his soul was seething and chaotic. She turned to her sewing again. But the sight of her bent before him held him and would not let him be. She was a strange, hostile, dominant thing. Yet not quite hostile. As he sat he felt his limbs were strong and hard, he sat in strength.

She was silent for a long time, stitching. He was aware, poignantly, of the round shape of her head, very intimate, compelling. She lifted her head and sighed. The blood burned in him, her voice ran to him like fire.

'Come here,' she said, unsure.

For some moments he did not move. Then he rose slowly and went across the hearth. It required an almost deathly effort of volition, or of acquiescence. He stood before her and looked down at her. Her face was shining again, her eyes were shining again like terrible laughter. It was to him terrible, how she could be transfigured. He could not look at her, it burnt his heart.

'My love!' she said.

And she put her arms round him as he stood before her, round his thighs, pressing him against her breast. And her hands on him seemed to reveal to him the mould of his own nakedness, he was passionately lovely to himself. He could not bear to look at her.

'My dear!' she said. He knew she spoke a foreign language. The fear was like bliss in his heart. He looked down. Her face was shining, her eyes were full of light, she was awful. He suffered from the compulsion to her. She was the awful unknown. He bent down to her, suffering, unable to let go, unable to let himself go, yet drawn, driven. She was now the transfigured, she was wonderful, beyond him. He wanted to go. But he could not as yet kiss her. He was himself apart. Easiest he could kiss her feet. But he was too ashamed for the actual deed, which were like an affront. She waited for him to meet her, not to bow before her and serve her. She wanted his active participation, not his submission. She put her fingers on him. And it was torture to him, that he must give himself to her actively, participate in her, that he must meet and embrace and know her, who was other than himself. There was that in him which shrank from yielding to her, resisted the relaxing towards her, opposed the mingling with her, even whilst he most desired it. He was afraid, he wanted to save himself.

There were a few moments of stillness. Then gradually, the tension, the withholding relaxed in him, and he began to flow towards her. She was beyond him, the unattainable. But he let go his hold on himself, he relinquished himself, and knew the subterranean force of his desire to come to her, to be with her, to mingle with her, losing himself to find her, to find himself in her. He began to approach her, to draw near.

His blood beat up in waves of desire. He wanted to come to her, to meet her. She was there, if he could reach her. The reality of her who was just beyond him absorbed him. Blind and destroyed, he pressed forward, nearer, nearer to receive the consummation of himself, be received within the darkness which should swallow him and yield him up to himself. If he could come really within the blazing kernel of darkness, if really he could be destroyed, burnt away till he lit with her in one consummation, that were supreme, supreme.[7]

This seems to me, without qualification, superior to any previous description of the development of a marriage relationship in the English novel. In its sense of the dialectical nature of love and hatred, of the contradictions and paradoxes which are the very essence of human relationships, such a passage is comparable only to the finest metaphysical poetry, to the lines, for instance, which conclude Donne's 'Holy Sonnet', 'Batter my heart, three person'd God'. My immediate point, however, is that the passage describing (or, better, conveying) the achievement of a happy, fulfilled relationship between Tom and Lydia ends with this sentence:

... Her father and her mother now met to the span of the heavens, and she, the child, was free to play in the space beneath, between.[8]

The image of the completed arch, symbolising a situation of positive and fulfilled harmony in which *all* the factors (not merely the sexual) of a complex whole meet creatively, this is the culmination of the first three chapters of the novel.

They are extraordinarily rich, these opening chapters, with their evocation of the Midlands scene, the countryside eaten into by the new industry, the curious, very English mingling of rural and urban. It has been well emphasised recently, especially by Dr Leavis and Professor Pinto, that Lawrence was far from being the rootless cosmopolitan which the wanderings of the latter part of his life suggest. As Professor Pinto has put it:

> ... Those who only know London and the south of England and Oxford and Cambridge tend to think of the Midlands merely as a grimy wilderness of ugliness and philistinism separating them from the Lake Country and Scotland. They may remember Matthew Arnold's remarks about provinciality and the dreariness of the Midland towns. What they ignore is not only the beauty of much of the Midland country, which, as we know well, is often found alongside ugliness and dreariness of the industrial areas, but also the existence of a great tradition of working-class and middle-class culture, which is just as real, and in some ways healthier and more vital than the gentlemanly tradition of the South. It is the tradition that shaped the genius of that great woman who wrote under the name of George Eliot in the nineteenth century, the old puritan tradition of provincial England, founded on the local church or chapel, the local elementary and secondary or grammar school and the local university or university college.[9]

This was Lawrence's background. It was ultimately the tragedy of his life that, owing partly to his deeply emotional relationship with his mother who was a petty-bourgeois woman, bitterly unsympathetic to and contemptuous of the working-class life into which her marriage pitched her, he failed to develop the possibility of achieving the freedom he sought through a more full participation in the aspirations and struggles of the people among whom he was born.

Even in these opening chapters of *The Rainbow* there are hints of that deep and treacherous snobbishness that was to destroy Lawrence; but it would be recklessly unjust to see these hints as the principal quality of the novel. Already the central theme is the bringing together of the inward and the outward life, the attempt to express and hence resolve the paradox that each human being is at once separate and yet a part of a whole, independent yet interdependent, a lone individual yet a social being.

At first it seems for a couple of pages as though Lawrence is going to postulate some kind of mystic union between man and nature, but the issues quickly become more complex and more valuable. Of the Brangwen woman he writes:

. . . She faced outwards to where men moved dominant and creative, having turned their back on the pulsing heat of creation, and with this behind them, were set out to discover what was beyond, to enlarge their own scope and range and freedom; whereas the Brangwen men faced inwards to the teeming life of creation, which poured unresolved into their veins.[10]

The profoundest issues are here invoked, the central problem of the novel achieving clarification. The mere acceptance and physical potency of the men are seen as inadequate, as holding back the fuller human aspirations of the race.

Looking out, as she must, from the front of her house towards the activity of man in the world at large, whilst her husband looked out to the back at sky and harvest and beast and land, she strained her eyes to see what man had done in fighting outwards to knowledge, she strained to hear how he uttered himself in his conquest, her deepest desire hung on the battle that she heard, far off, being waged on the edge of the unknown. She also wanted to know, and to be of the fighting host.[11]

'The activity of man in the world at large.' It is presented as the other side of the coin, the aspect of human life without which the satisfaction of personal physical needs is meaningless and impossible. Pounding through *The Rainbow* is this double sense—the sense of man as a unique individual faced with choices upon which depend his ability to develop his potentialities and the sense of man as a social being, a part of a larger whole, faced with the universe and striving to master it. The search, the passionate, desperate search of the characters of *The Rainbow* is to achieve personal relationships which make them at one with the universe, to overcome the apparent contradiction between the individual and the social being.

There are introduced in the course of the novel a number of un-satisfactory attempts at resolution, false arches which fail, despite appearances, to link the innermost with the universe. One is nature itself: the community which the early, farming Brangwens feel with the earth's processes, the arch of trees under which Ursula temporarily seeks shelter from the storm in the final chapter. Another is the world of science—'the area under an arc lamp . . .

lit up by man's completest consciousness'[12]—which Ursula as a student at Nottingham for a moment submits to but soon rejects. More important is the Church.

The Church is the most fully explored false arch in *The Rainbow*. It is introduced as something very near a symbol in the first paragraph of the novel.

Whenever one of the Brangwens in the fields lifted his head from his work, he saw the church-tower at Ilkeston in the empty sky. So that as he turned again to the horizontal land, he was aware of something standing above him and beyond him in the distance.[13]

The possibility of the Church as the rainbow is here explicitly suggested and the theme is returned to many times throughout the novel, but particularly in the chapter 'The Cathedral' in which the significance of Lincoln Cathedral to Will Brangwen is revealed.

Away from time, always outside of time! Between east and west, between dawn and sunset, the church lay like a seed in silence, dark before germination, silenced after death. Containing birth and death, potential with all the noise and transitation of life, the cathedral remained hushed, a great, involved seed, whereof the flower would be radiant life inconceivable but whose beginning and whose end were the circle of silence. Spanned round with the rainbow, the jewelled gloom folded music upon silence, light upon darkness, fecundity upon death, as a seed folds leaf upon leaf and silence upon the root and the flower, hushing up the secret of all between its parts, the death out of which it fell, the life into which it has dropped, the immortality it involves, and the death it will embrace again.[14]

This is to Will a satisfactory consummation of his needs. 'There his soul remained, at the apex of the arch, clinched in the timeless ecstasy, consummated.' But to Anna it is an empty answer, though she feels for a time the force of it. 'She claimed the right to freedom above her, higher than the roof.' The Church does not embrace the whole of the universe; its pretensions are ultimately bogus.

The final vision of the rainbow by Ursula is tentative and, one is bound to say, mystical. It is clear, by the end of the novel, what she had rejected, less clear what she still hopes for. She has rejected Skrebensky—beautiful, animal, but conventional, the servant of the imperial state,[15] lacking inwardness and an understanding of the profounder aspirations of the soul. With less difficulty she has rejected Winifred Inger and her cynical uncle Tom, physically and spiritually corrupt. She has turned her back with distaste upon modern industrial society—'a dry brittle, terrible corruption spreading over the face of the land'—and the church 'standing up in hideous obsoleteness'. Social service in the form of her work as a teacher she has rejected as barren and useless. Nothing remains but a vague, insistent conviction (Lawrence's own) that somehow or other men will come through, achieve some kind of rebirth in which full, potent lives and mutually satisfactory relationships will again be possible.

This then is the 'message' of *The Rainbow*, the burden of the book which Lawrence wrote, and of no writer does the word burden hold a more thorough-going significance. It is a common criticism of Lawrence and, I think, on the whole a just one that the intensity of his novels is to some extent self-destructive, that his characters live at a pitch of intensity which is not only uncommon in experience but altogether disproportionate. It is perhaps important therefore to insist on the range and flow of interest invoked in *The Rainbow*, the amount of 'life' upon which the intensity of emotion within the book is, so to speak, exercised.

Because of the intensity, the way in which the climaxes of individual relationships are presented, we tend to think of Lawrence's characters and situations as almost—despite the often obsessive concern with the physical and sexual reactions—disembodied, units of vital matter whirling and clashing in a vast dark universe in which time and place are of little relevance or even reality. It is important to try to assess how far this impression is a just one and how far it comes from an unfamiliarity with Lawrence's technique.

If one attempts to sum up the range of experience and interest involved in *The Rainbow* it turns out to be very large indeed. There is the whole question of the relationship between work and personality; there is an examination of the social set-up of Cossethay and Beldover, the position of the squire and the vicar and the schoolmaster; there is the problem of industrialisation, the significance of the canal and the railway and the pits; there is a great deal and from many points of view about the English educational system; there is the question of the impact of the English Midlands on the Polish *émigrés*; above all there is all that is implied in the phrase 'the emancipation of women'. Such issues, abstracted as 'issues', may seem at first to have little enough to do with the impact of the novel. In fact, I believe, *The Rainbow* is far more securely rooted in reality, far more concretely based in the actual human, social issues of twentieth-century England than many readers recognise.

It is tempting, for instance (and Lawrence himself often gives us excuse enough) to think of Lawrence's psychological interest as being rather abstract. In fact, one has only to recall his descriptions of childhood in this novel to realise the injustice of the impression. The extraordinary poignancy as well as the power of the description of Anna's misery when she is kept from her mother who is having another child or the conveying of the relationship between Will and the baby Ursula, such achievements of art have nothing theoretic, nothing abstract about them. If a technical knowledge of psychology as a 'subject' lies behind them it is a knowledge that has been fully absorbed into an ordered consciousness.

The Rainbow, I have said, is securely rooted in reality. At its best it is a revelation of the nature of personal relationships in twentieth-century England of incomparable power and insight. Lawrence's vision of bourgeois society is indeed so potent, so devastating in its uncompromising horror that it was inevitable that the book should outrage the upholders of law and order.* The usual assessment of the novel, that it begins superbly and then declines, is less than true. Certainly the opening chapters, culminating in the achievement of happiness by Tom and Lydia, are done with great insight and richness, but they are also, in comparison with the later reaches of the book, uncomplex. The full significance of the coming of the canal (serving the new collieries) has not yet become clear, though it is by more than chance that the bursting of the canal-bank kills Tom Brangwen. The relationship of Tom and Lydia, though it is not conceived at all in pastoral terms, is uncomplicated by the issues which are to prove too much for their grandchild Ursula and the second generation Polish *émigré*, Skrebensky. Fundamentally it is a pre-capitalist relationship between a successful working farmer and the daughter of a feudal landowner and its fulfilment is bound up with a sense of oneness with nature and a simple social set-up which is largely off the track of the developing society. 'Immune' is significantly a word which Anna returns to several times when she is looking back later on her life at the Marsh.

Compared with the world the later generations have to face, the world of the Marsh is almost idyllic. Will and Anna fight out their battle in more desperate terms but with them the implications at stake are still muffled because fundamentally both capitulate, losing sight of the rainbow and ending in their modern house at

* In October 1915 *The Rainbow* was declared obscene and the magistrates ordered the recall and destruction of all copies.

Beldover, respectable and defeated, happy only in the second-rate happiness of a dishonest compromise. Anna Victrix will end her life as something very like a complacent suburban matron.

It is Ursula, from the moment she—literally—reaches for the moon and then later sallies forth into the man's world, who is brought, like Lawrence himself, up against the full reality of the bourgeois world. The last chapters of *The Rainbow* seem to me not, artistically, finer than the first but more moving, more courageous, more fully relevant to the twentieth-century world.

In her aspiration towards freedom Ursula faces facts which neither Lydia nor Anna have had to face. The most important of them—though by no means all—are involved in her relationship with Skrebensky. Even in the early stages of their relationship it is clear that he will, unless he can achieve a transformation against which the odds are stacked, fail her.

There is an important passage in the eleventh chapter ('First Love') in which the young Skrebensky discusses his life with Ursula.

Ursula and Anton Skrebensky walked along the ridge of the canal between. The berries on the hedges were crimson and bright red, above the leaves. The glow of evening and the wheeling of the solitary pee-wit and the faint cry of the birds came to meet the shuffling noise of the pits, the dark, fuming stress of the town opposite, and they two walked the blue strip of water-way, the ribbon of sky between.

He was looking, Ursula thought, very beautiful, because of a flush of sunburn on his hands and face. He was telling her how he had learned to shoe horses and select cattle fit for killing.

'Do you like to be a soldier?' she asked.

'I am not exactly a soldier,' he replied.

'But you only do things for wars,' she said.

'Yes.'

'Would you like to go to war?'

'I? Well, it would be exciting. If there were a war I would want to go.'

A strange, distracted feeling came over her, a sense of potent unrealities.

'Why would you want to go?'

'I should be doing something, it would be genuine. It's a sort of toy-life as it is.'

'But what would you be doing if you went to war?'

'I would be making railways or bridges, working like a nigger.'

'But you'd only make them to be pulled down again when the armies had done with them. It seems just as much a game.'

'If you call war a game.'

'What is it?'

'It's about the most serious business there is, fighting.'

A sense of hard separateness came over her.

'Why is fighting more serious than anything else?' she asked.

'You either kill or get killed—and I suppose it is serious enough, killing.'

'But when you're dead you don't matter any more,' she said.

He was silent for a moment.

'But the result matters,' he said. 'It matters whether we settle the Mahdi or not.'

'Not to you—nor me—we don't care about Khartoum.'

'You want to have room to live in: and somebody has to make room.'

'But I don't want to live in the desert of Sahara—do you?' she replied, laughing with antagonism.

'I don't—but we've got to back up those who do.'

'Why have we?'

'Where is the nation if we don't?'

'But we aren't the nation. There are heaps of other people who are the nation.'

'They might say *they* weren't either.'

'Well, if everybody said it, there wouldn't be a nation. But I should still be myself,' she asserted brilliantly.

'You wouldn't be yourself if there were no nation.'

'Why not?'

'Because you'd just be a prey to everybody and anybody.'

'How a prey?'

'They'd come and take everything you'd got.'

'Well, they couldn't take much even then. I don't care what they take. I'd rather have a robber who carried me off than a millionaire who gave me everything you can buy.'

'That's because you are a romanticist.'

'Yes, I am. I want to be romantic. I hate houses that never go away, and people just living in the houses. It's all so stiff and stupid. I hate soldiers, they are stiff and wooden. What do you fight for, really?'

'I would fight for the nation.'

'For all that, you aren't the nation. What would you do for yourself?'

'I belong to the nation and must do my duty by the nation.'

'But when it didn't need your services in particular—when there *is* no fighting? What would you do then?'

He was irritated.

'I would do what everybody else does.'

'What?'

'Nothing. I would be in readiness for when I was needed.'

The answer came in exasperation.

'It seems to me,' she answered, 'as if you weren't anybody—as if there weren't anybody there, where you are. Are you anybody, really? You seem like nothing to me.[16]

Nothing could better convey a sense of the futility of the conventional middle-class young man's life, and the passage is followed by the memorable incident in which Ursula gives her necklace and her name to the barge-people's baby, an act whose significance Skrebensy totally fails to understand. 'The woman had been a servant, I'm sure of that' is all he can say. Well might Ursula wince.

When later they become lovers it is still the same. Save his physical beauty the young man has almost nothing to give Ursula. His values are the values of the Indian army sahib and his consolation is the same—whisky. And because of his limitations he cannot love Ursula though he wants to desperately. To Lawrence love that is merely sexual is in the long run valueless. It is the total human being he is concerned with and what shocked him about contemporary society was what it did to the total human being.

To be alive, to be man alive, to be whole man alive: that is the point. And at its best, the novel, and the novel supremely can help you.[17]

It is worth recalling the recurrence of the theme of 'living' in Henry James, particularly the famous passage in *The Ambassadors* in which Strether talks to little Bilham: 'Live all you can; it's a mistake not to. . . .'[18] Lawrence and James are, superficially, extremely contrasted writers, yet we shall find, I believe, that the value of the work of both lies ultimately in this passionate striving after life and the sense in both that the world into which they and their characters are pitched denies the potentialities of living. It is this positive sense of human aspiration which goes so far to counteract the unsatisfactory—and indeed life-denying—elements in their own philosophies.

In James, as we have seen, the destructive element within the novels may be isolated as a very sophisticated kind of aestheticism, a particular delight in situations in which the seeker after life is trapped and forced towards death. In Lawrence the danger-point is the Lawrentian brand of mysticism, a mysticism which it is difficult to define without doing Lawrence an injustice, but which nevertheless permeates his writing.

It is not quite fair to saddle Lawrence with some of his wilder statements about the superiority of the blood over the intellect. Such statements, especially out of context, are belied by the total impact of his work which does not have the effect of doing down the intelligence. And yet it must be recognised that there is something not merely unsatisfactory but positively pernicious within

such a novel as *The Rainbow*. It can perhaps best be indicated by
the attitude not simply of Ursula Brangwen but of Lawrence himself towards ordinary working people. The theme of *The Rainbow*
is what bourgeois society does to personal relationships. The pledge
of *The Rainbow* is that a new society will come about in which men
and women will be able to live whole and achieve vital, creative
relationships. But the relation of the theme to the pledge, of the
earth to the rainbow, is shrouded in wordiness and mysticism.

The root of the problem is Lawrence's own identification of
democracy with bourgeois democracy and society with bourgeois
society. It is this identification which forces him, in his search for
a positive hope, into the swamps of mysticism. We have already
seen how, in his brilliant analysis of *The Forsyte Saga*, he equates
the word 'social' with 'acquisitive'. There is a passage towards the
end of *The Rainbow* which is equally significant, not merely because
it throws light on Lawrence's political views (that is not the point),
but because it contains one of the clearest indications of the un-
solved contradiction which wreaks havoc with the latter part of
the novel as a work of art. Ursula and Skrebensky are talking of
their projected marriage:

Once she said, with heat:
'I shall be glad to leave England. Everything is so meagre and paltry,
it is so unspiritual—I hate democracy.'
He became angry to hear her talk like this, he did not know why.
Somehow, he could not bear it, when she attacked things. It was as if
she were attacking him.
'What do you mean?' he asked her, hostile. 'Why do you hate demo-
cracy?'
'Only the greedy and ugly people come to the top in a democracy,'
she said, 'because they're the only people who will push themselves there.
Only degenerate races are democratic.'
'What do you want then—an aristocracy?' he asked, secretly moved.
He always felt that by rights he belonged to the ruling aristocracy. Yet
to hear her speak for his class pained him with a curious, painful pleasure.
He felt he was aquiescing in something illegal, taking to himself some
wrong, reprehensible advantage.
'I *do* want an aristocracy,' she cried. 'And I'd far rather have an aristo-
cracy of birth than of money. Who are the aristocrats now—who are
chosen as the best to rule? Those who have money and the brains for
money. It doesn't matter what else they have: but they must have money-
brains—because they are ruling in the name of money.'
'The people elect the government,' he said.
'I know they do. But what are the people? Each one of them is a

money interest. I hate it, that anybody is my equal who has the same amount of money as I have. I *know* I am better than all of them. I hate them. They are not my equals. I hate equality on a money basis. It is the equality of dirt.'

Her eyes blazed at him, he felt as if she wanted to destroy him. She had gripped him and was trying to break him. His anger sprang up, against her. At least he would fight for his existence with her. A hard, blind resistance possessed him.

'*I* don't care about money,' he said, 'neither do I want to put my finger in the pie. I am too sensitive about my finger.'

'What is your finger to me?' she cried, in a passion. 'You with your dainty fingers, and your going to India because you will be one of the somebodies there! It's a mere dodge, your going to India.'

'In what way a dodge?' he cried, white with anger and fear.

'You think the Indians are simpler than us, and so you'll enjoy being near them and being a lord over them,' she said. 'And you'll feel so righteous, governing them for their own good. Who are you, to feel righteous? What are you righteous about, in your governing? Your governing stinks. What do you govern for, but to make things there as dead and mean as they are here!'

'I don't feel righteous in the least,' he said.

'Then what *do* you feel? It's all such a nothingness, what you feel and what you don't feel.'

'What do you feel yourself?' he asked. 'Aren't you righteous in your own mind?'

'Yes, I am, because I'm against you, and all your old, dead things,' she cried.[19]

It is a very subtle passage. The indictment of Skrebensky could scarcely be more shrewd or more profound from any point of view, psychological or social. And in Ursula's anger the whole of Lawrence's hatred and contempt of bourgeois society comes through. Yet there is also something very deep in Ursula's own attitude which prevents her from being able to cope adequately with Skrebensky. Her identification of the people with 'a money interest' disarms her. That it should disarm her as a debater doesn't of course matter (no one need demand that Ursula must, in a theoretical sense, be 'right'). What does matter is that it disarms her as an active agent in the novel and hands her over to an orgy of mystical clap-trap. Since Ursula is at this point carrying on her shoulders all of the positives of the novel—it is she who is about to achieve the vision of the rainbow—it matters intensely that these positives should be given no coherent, concrete expression. It means, among other things, that the final image of the rainbow, upon which almost everything, artistically, must depend, is not a triumphant image resolving in itself the half-clarified contradictions brought into play throughout the book, but a misty, vague and unrealised vision which gives us no more than the general sense that Lawrence is, after all, on the side of life.

There are, I think, two ways in which Lawrence's unsatisfatory philosophy seriously limits the success and value of *The Rainbow* as a work of art. In the first place, there is the excessive intensity, the lack of relaxation, which gives the book as a whole an obsessive quality, all rather high-pitched and overwrought. In the second place—not quite separable from this first quality—is the unresolved element of mysticism. In the final pages of the book Lawrence seems to be making a desperate effort to slough off this mysticism, to purge from his vision its excessive individualism, to see his people not in terms of mysterious allotropic states of being, but as men and women born and living and struggling in twentieth-century England, nowhere else.

Ursula's temptation to see the world as unreality is clearly stated:

Repeatedly, in an ache of utter weariness she repeated:
'I have no father nor mother nor lover, I have no allocated place in the world of things, I do not belong to Beldover nor to Nottingham nor to England nor to this world, they none of them exist, I am trammelled and entangled in them, but they are unreal. I must break out of it, like a nut from its shell which is an unreality.'

But the temptation is rejected and the rainbow finally appears standing upon the earth.

She knew that Skrebensky had never become finally real. In the weeks of passionate ecstasy he had been with her in her desire, she had created him for the time being. But in the end he had failed and broken down.

Strange, what a void separated him and her. She liked him now, as she liked a memory, some bygone self. He was something of the past, finite. He was that which is known. She felt a poignant affection for him, as for that which is past. But, when she looked ahead, into the un-discovered land before her, what was there she could recognise but a fresh glow of light and inscrutable trees going up from the earth like smoke. It was the unknown, the unexplored, the undiscovered upon whose shore she had landed, alone, after crossing the void, the darkness which washed the New World and the Old.

There would be no child: she was glad. If there had been a child, it would have made little difference, however. She would have kept the child and herself, she would not have gone to Skrebensky. Anton belonged to the past.

There came the cablegram from Skrebensky. 'I am married.' An old pain and anger and contempt stirred in her. Did he belong so utterly to the cast-off past? She repudiated him. He was as he was. It was good that he was as he was. Who was she to have a man according to her own desire? It was not for her to create, but to recognise a man created by God. The man should come from the Infinite and she should hail him. She was glad she could not create her man. She was glad that this lay within the scope of that vaster power in which she rested at last. The man would come out of Eternity to which she herself belonged.

As she grew better, she sat to watch a new creation. As she sat at her window, she saw the people go by in the street below, colliers, women, children, walking each in the husk of an old fruition, but visible through the husk, the swelling and the heaving contour of the new germination. In the still, silenced forms of the colliers she saw a sort of suspense, a waiting in pain for the new liberation; she saw the same in the false hard confidence of the women. The confidence of the women was brittle. It would break quickly to reveal the strength and patient effort of the new germination.

In everything she saw she grasped and groped to find the creation of the living God, instead of the old, hard barren form of bygone living. Sometimes great terror possessed her. Sometimes she lost touch, she lost her feeling, she could only know the old horror of the husk which bound in her and all mankind. They were all in prison, they were all going mad.

She saw the stiffened bodies of the colliers, which seemed already enclosed in a coffin, she saw their unchanging eyes, the eyes of those who are buried alive: she saw the hard, cutting edges of the new houses, which seemed to spread over the hillside in their insentient triumph, the triumph of horrible, amorphous angles and straight lines, the expression of corruption triumphant and unopposed, corruption so pure that it is hard and brittle: she saw the dun atmosphere over the blackened hills opposite, the dark blotches of houses, slate roofed and amorphous, the old church-tower standing up in hideous obsoleteness above raw new houses on the crest of the hill, the amorphous, brittle, hard-edged new houses advancing from Beldover to meet the corrupt new houses from Lethley, the houses of Lethley advancing to mix with the houses of Hainor, a dry, brittle, terrible corruption spreading over the face of the land, and she was sick with a nausea so deep that she perished as she sat. And then, in the blowing clouds, she saw a band of faint iridescence colouring in faint colours a portion of the hill. And forgetting, startled, she looked for the hovering colour and saw a rainbow forming itself. In one place it gleamed fiercely, and, her heart anguished with hope, she sought the shadow of iris where the bow should be. Steadily the colour gathered, mysteriously, from nowhere, it took presence upon itself, there was a faint, vast rainbow. The arc bended and strengthened itself till it arched indomitable, making great architecture of light and colour and the space of heaven, its pedestals luminous in the corruption of new houses on the low hill, its arch the top of heaven.

And the rainbow stood on the earth. She knew that the sordid people who crept hard-scaled and separate on the face of the world's corruption were living still, that the rainbow was arched in their blood and would quiver to life in their spirit, that they would cast off their horny covering of disintegration, that new, clean, naked bodies would issue to a new germination, to a new growth, rising to the light and the wind and the clean rain of heaven. She saw in the rainbow the earth's new architecture, the old, brittle corruption of houses and factories swept away, the world built up in a living fabric of Truth, fitting to the over-arching heaven.[20]

Reality and mysticism battle into the very last sentences of the book. Lawrence's hatred of factories fights with his realisation of the need of them; his sense of man's separateness struggles with his rejection of separateness, his contempt of the people with his love of them. He cannot resolve the contradictions.

5

JAMES JOYCE: ULYSSES

(1922)

James Joyce, unlike D. H. Lawrence, was an aesthete, an artist chasing the chimera of a complete, abstracted aesthetic experience. Stephen Dedalus, in a conversation which is one of the central episodes in *A Portrait of the Artist as a Young Man* (1916), says:

'. . . Beauty expressed by the artist cannot awaken in us an emotion that is kinetic or a sensation which is purely physical. It awakens, or ought to awaken, or induces, or ought to induce, an aesthetic stasis, an ideal pity or an ideal terror, a stasis called forth, prolonged, and at last dissolved by what I call the rhythm of beauty.'

'What is that exactly?' asked Lynch.

'Rhythm,' said Stephen, 'is the first formal aesthetic relation of part to part in any aesthetic whole or of an aesthetic whole to its part or parts or of any part to the aesthetic whole of which it is a part.'

'If that is rhythm,' said Lynch, 'let me hear what you call beauty; and please remember, that though I did eat a cake of cowdung once, that I admire only beauty.'

Stephen raised his cap as if in greeting. Then, blushing slightly, he laid his hand on Lynch's thick tweed sleeve.

'We are right,' he said, 'and the others are wrong. To speak of these things and to try to understand their nature and, having understood it, to try slowly and humbly and constantly to express, to press out again, from the gross earth or what it brings forth, from sound and shape and colour which are the prison gates of our soul, an image of the beauty we have come to understand—that is art.'[1]

It is a passage relevant in a number of ways—including even the cowdung—to an approach to *Ulysses*.

The subject of *Ulysses* is sometimes described in some such terms as 'the record of a single day, June 16th, 1904' or 'twenty-four hours in the life of a modern city'. I do not think the emphasis here is quite right. Dublin is the scene, and in a sense the be-all of Joyce's book; yet *Ulysses* is not *about* Dublin any more than Homer's *Odyssey* is about the places Odysseus visits. The subject of *Ulysses* is the odyssey of Leopold Bloom and, since no man is an island, his relationships with other human beings, of which the most important are, obviously, his wife Molly and Stephen Dedalus.

Ulysses, although quite clearly a unique work and in some respects a revolutionary development in the novel as art-form, is in one of the main traditions of the English novel. Fielding's famous description of *Joseph Andrews*, 'a comic epic poem in prose', fits it better perhaps than any other twentieth-century novel. It has the scale and scope and even—despite the misty vapour at its heart—something of the objectivity of epic, and it is at the same time, like *Don Quixote*, mock-epic, essentially comic in its underlying approach. So much rather heavy solemnity surrounds the bulk of the discussion of *Ulysses* that it is perhaps worth emphasising right away that it is a very funny novel, including passages as uproarious as anything in modern fiction.

Another point worth making concerns the novel's 'difficulty'. Because of Joyce's extraordinary virtuosity, the wealth of references and allusions that are, to most reader's intents and purposes, un-traceable, and the eccentric texture of certain passages, this 'difficulty' has, I think, been exaggerated. Any reader who can cope with, say, a Shakespeare play or *Tristram Shandy*, will not find the bulk of *Ulysses* excessively difficult. There will no doubt be points that he misses (this is true of the most conscientious attacker) and passages he finds obscure, but this will not prevent him from getting to the heart of the book nor from enjoying most of the incidental felicities. Such passages as the opening of the Siren episode, which Mr Levin has usefully elucidated,[2] need not be grasped in their every detail for the essential point to be taken, nor need one have more than a vague knowledge of what is being paro-died to get the essential hang of the hospital scene. It is probably well to read *Ulysses* fairly fast; much of the complex system of cross-reference then falls more or less naturally into place.*

* One can, for instance, appreciate the lunch-bar episode perfectly adequately without being conscious that 'the technic of this episode is based on a process of nutrition: *peristalsis*, "the automatic muscular movement consisting of wave-like contractions in successive circles by which nutritive matter is propelled along the alimentary canal". This process is symbolised by Mr Bloom's pauses before various

How important is the relation of *Ulysses* to the Homeric epic? Much has been written on this subject and a good many parallels drawn which to the average reader must seem far-fetched and unhelpful. Although *Ulysses* is a mock-epic it certainly does not stand in the kind of relation to Homer that *Don Quixote* does to the chivalric romances. Joyce, particularly while he was living in Switzerland, where much of *Ulysses* was written, was soaked in the atmosphere of contemporary psychological research and its resultant cults. I do not know if Joyce should be called a Jungian, but to say that he looked upon the Homeric epic in the light of an archetype, a symbolic expression of certain patterns of human experience of universal and almost mystical significance, seems a fair assessment of his attitude.

It is true that in *Ulysses* Joyce does to some extent use the contrast between a glamorous, heroic and integrated past and a sordid, unheroic, disintegrating present as a source of irony (that Bloom is not a hero is an essential point about him; heroes do not fear piles or passively accept Penelope's infidelities) just as it is in T. S. Eliot's *Waste Land*; but the irony is in both cases double-edged, it reduces the past as well as the present. The chief point of the Homeric parallel is that it provides a framework which—given the authority of Homer plus the theory of archetypes—strengthens the illusion of an underlying pattern of the deepest significance. As a matter of fact Joyce is prepared to dabble in any kind of myth, quite apart from the *Odyssey*, which will contribute to this illusion. The *Wandering Jew* and the Eternal Feminine are grist to his mill. This said, it remains true that a realisation that the basic structure of *Ulysses* is related to that of the *Odyssey*, that Bloom is Odysseus, Stephen Telemachus and Molly Penelope, is necessary to an intelligent reading of the book and not more than a novelist is justified in demanding of his reader. There is, emphatically, no need to make heavy weather of the more abstruse Homeric parallels.

The first three sections, or chapters, of *Ulysses* are a kind of elaborate lead-in to the book proper. They form, moreover, a significant bridge between *A Portrait of the Artist* and the infinitely more ambitious *Ulysses*. Stephen remains the chief character though he is presented rather more objectively than in the *Portrait*. That work, concerned above all with his struggle to emancipate himself from the Roman Catholic Church, had ended with his

places of refreshment, the incomplete movements he makes towards the satisfaction of the pangs of hunger which spasmodically urge him onward and their ultimate appeasement. . . .'[3]

decision to become—it is a keyword throughout Joyce—an exile. At the climax of the very moving conversation with Cranly his vow of *non serviam* (the devil's vow) is made.

'Look here, Cranly,' he said. 'You have asked me what I would do and what I would not do. I will tell you what I will do and what I will not do. I will not serve that in which I no longer believe, whether it call itself my home, my fatherland or my church: and I will try to express myself in some mode of life or art as freely as I can and as wholly as I can, using for my weapons the only arms I allow myself to use—silence, exile and cunning.'[4]

It is the apotheosis of individualism, a rejection of obligation social and religious so complete that the later, somewhat shrill pledge, 'Welcome, O Life! I go to encounter for the millionth time the reality of experience and to forge in the smithy of my soul the un-created conscience of my race',[5] rings false and melodramatic. For what's his race to Stephen or an exile to Ireland?

The Stephen of *Ulysses* has returned to Dublin from Paris, summoned home for his mother's death. From the very first pages of the book the situation in which he finds himself—he has refused the dying wish of his mother and is haunted by his decision—becomes a leading theme of the novel, one of the recurring leit-motifs which give it its unity. For the rejection of his mother is not merely a personal thing but bound up with his rejection of Church and State—'the imperial British state and the holy Roman catholic and apostolic church'.[6] Stephen's part in the book is indeed that of the Son. He is Telemachus and Japhet, searching for a father. He is an Irishman rejecting Britain which is associated through the sea (the Englishman is 'the seas' ruler') with the mother (the sea is 'our mighty mother'). Equally he rejects Ireland, the milkwoman, also a mother-symbol but with 'old, shrunken paps'. He is Hamlet, he is the erring son of the Church, he is, blasphemously, through the rape of the mother by the panther (it was, we learn, Panther the Roman centurion who violated the Virgin Mary), Jesus.

Leopold Bloom is, equally, the Father searching for his Son—his only actual son died at the age of eleven days—and is through-out the book in some mysterious *rapport* with Stephen though they do not actually meet to speak until well into the last half of the novel. The coming-together of Bloom and Stephen in the brothel scene, culminating in the moment when Bloom, standing over the prostrate Stephen, has a vision of his dead son, is the climax of the book.

We shall have to return later to a consideration of this frame-work of *Ulysses*, the pattern which gives the total book what unity it possesses; meanwhile it will be necessary to say something about Joyce's technical methods.

A great deal of *Ulysses* is written in the form of a kind of short-hand impressionism which aims to convey the thought-track of the characters.

On the doorstep he felt in his hip-pocket for the latchkey. Not there. In the trousers I left off. Must get it. Potato I have. Creaky wardrobe. No use disturbing her. She turned over sleepily that time. He pulled the halldoor to after him very quietly, more, till the footleaf dropped gently over the threshold, a limp lid. Looked shut. All right till I come back anyhow.[7]

It has become almost a parlour-game among commentators to find precedents for this method and already Shakespeare, Richardson, Fanny Burney, Dickens, Fenimore Cooper and Samuel Butler have been cited among the ancestors of the work to which Joyce himself admitted his indebtedness—*Les Lauriers sont coupés* by Edouard Dujardin. The truth is that any writer who has attempted to indicate in the first person something of the thought-processes of his characters is likely to write some form of interior monologue and Joyce, until the final chapter of *Ulysses*, is original largely in the extent to which he uses the method. Two points should perhaps be noted. In the first place what Joyce is doing in passages like the short one quoted above is not to limit the point of view to that of the particular character he is dealing with. He is not primarily con-cerned to show life through the eyes of Bloom. Rather he is using Bloom's impressions to add a dimension and enrich the texture of an objective description of reality. Hence objective statements in the third person ('he felt in his hip-pocket for the latchkey') are intermingled with unspoken soliloquy ('In the trousers I left off'). In the second place we should recognise that the attempt to give an impression of a thought-track is indeed impressionist and not 'scientific'. Joyce does not succeed any more than any other writer in finding a precise verbal equivalent for unformulated thoughts, as indeed, by the nature of things, he cannot. Such a phrase as 'Potato I have' serves its purpose. The thought 'I have a hole in my pocket like a potato' is expressed in a way which, by its very waywardness and obliquity, gives a certain illusion of thought-processes, but its real value in Joyce's scheme is that it can and will

be used as a minor leitmotif, a recurring phrase associated with
the loss of Bloom's front-door key (keys themselves having a
major symbolic significance throughout *Ulysses*) and his relations
with his wife. Five hundred pages later Bloom will ask one of the
whores in the brothel to give him back his potato.

> BLOOM:
> There is a memory attached to it. I should like to have it.
> STEPHEN:
> To have or not to have, that is the question.
> ZOE:
> Here. (*She hauls up a reef of her slip, revealing her bare thigh and unrolls
> the potato from the top of her stocking.*) Those that hides knows where
> to find.[8]

The tiny episode illustrates, perhaps, something of Joyce's method
and the levels of suggestion upon which he simultaneously works.
In the first place the scene is at once farcical and sordid, trivial and
significant. 'There is a memory attached to it': the phrase is at once
a cliché and a revelation. The whole paraphernalia of cheap sentimentality ('Thanks for the memory', etc.) of escapist entertainment
is conjured up, Zoe becoming for a second that familiar figure the
can-can girl, the predecessor of the strip-tease artiste (*sic*) who
symbolises the pornographic character of such culture ('Why,
strip-tease without music ain't art'). And the psychological situation behind the brothel-world is at the same time suggested in a
number of ways. Bloom is not wicked in an abstract sense, he is
sentimental and frustrated. 'I should like to have it' refers of course
not simply to the potato but to his wife. Stephen's parody of
Hamlet makes us pause on the reiterated word 'have' and its associations. Indirectly it brings in—and because the profundity of
Hamlet's soliloquy is immediately invoked we take up the cue—
the complex relationships between thought and action ('letting I
dare not wait upon I will') acquisitiveness and sex-relations. There
is nothing heavy or pompous in the method of this association.
Stephen's intervention is ridiculous as well as relevant. Stephen-
Hamlet is no more master of the situation than Bloom or, for that
matter, Zoe, who will shortly be put in her place by the ubiquitous
madame of the brothel, Bella Cohen, simultaneously male and
female, Jew and gentile, a Circe who threatens at the critical moment
(a superb shaft of irony) to call the police.

'Those that hides knows where to find' might well sometimes
be said of Joyce's own method of cross-reference and it is worth

noticing that the images and phrases especially associated with a particular character's 'stream of consciousness' crop up from time to time in the interior monologue of somebody else. 'The corpse-chewer! Raw head and bloody bones!'[9] cries Stephen as the figure of his mother appears to him in the brothel scene and we are taken back not only to the long series of richly complex images surrounding Stephen's own riddle ('a pard, a panther, got in spouse-breach, vulturing the dead') but to the butcher's shop that Bloom has patronised earlier in the day. What Joyce is attempting in fact is not the mere conveying of a character's impressions but a radical extension, exploiting all the ambiguities of language, of the normal methods of objective description.

The intricate system of leitmotif which Joyce developed—his methods of composition apparently involved something like a card-index system with coloured crayons to assist the process—has its own value in the achievement of a remarkable richness and complexity of texture, as complex often as life itself. As Mr Levin has well put it:

> He did not bring literature any closer to life than perceptive novelists had already done; he did evolve his private mode of rhetorical discourse. He sought to illuminate the mystery of consciousness, and he ended by developing a complicated system of literary leitmotive.[10]

The final chapter of *Ulysses* is of course in a rather different category. Here, with the abandonment of punctuation, there seems to be a more consistent attempt actually to reproduce the stream of consciousness. The thoughts are now no longer broken by objective statements in the third person, they glide on and into each other until consciousness is finally overcome by sleep. It must be remembered that the lack of any kind of objective statement in this chapter is made possible only by the peculiar moment of consciousness Joyce has here chosen to communicate. Molly Bloom's thoughts need no punctuation because, lying in bed, action has been eliminated. The cross-play of thought and action is no longer a technical problem. It is significant that the stream of consciousness method can only come into play in its purest form when consciousness is no longer an active apprehension of the present but a mode of recollection and impulse divorced from actual activity. I think a great deal too much has been made by critics of Molly Bloom's final affirmation. What reason have we to suppose that it will stand the test of tomorrow morning's reality? In any case it is doubtful whether it has been induced by more than a casual—and scarcely productive—recollection. I do not think there is really any progression in *Ulysses*. Those who have called its construction circular are nearer the truth.

What, then, are some of the reasons for regarding *Ulysses* as something more than a virtuoso piece, an astonishing but ultimately rather absurd phenomenon which manages paradoxically to combine the qualities of the cul-de-sac and the endless journey?

In the first place there is Joyce's remarkable ability to bring a scene to life. *Ulysses*, despite some exasperating qualities and passages, tingles with life, with the physical feel of existence and with a sense of the vibrating reality of human relationships. I cannot think of any finer expression of the 'feel' of the comparatively early morning than the opening pages of *Ulysses*. The kind of effect that Hardy achieves in the fields of Talbothays Joyce gets on a far more complex scale—the scale of sophisticated urban as opposed to rural peasant life—and he gets it by immediately setting in motion the disparate consciousnesses of Buck Mulligan, Stephen and, later, Haines. Mulligan's full-blooded and unscrupulous blasphemies are rather like gong-blows picking up echoes and gathering distortions as their vibrations encounter differing surfaces. The early exchanges between Stephen and Mulligan and Haines, stating as they do so many of the essential themes of the book, get their effect not from the intrinsic interest of the intellectual arguments involved, though this is often considerable, but from the human situation, general and personal, behind the arguments.

It is the same in all the best passages of the book. The immediate physical sense we get of Molly Bloom lying drowsily in bed, of the movement in the streets, of Davy Burne's lunch bar, of the cabman's shelter, of the three-master gliding into port, all is achieved with a relaxation of art, a cunning play on rhythmical detail, a supremely subtle sense of language.

> He turned his face over a shoulder, rere regardant. Moving through the air high spars of a three master, her sails brailed up on the crosstrees, homing, upstream, silently moving, a silent ship.[11]

The effect is got by a number of touches. Stephen is moving, so is the ship and that he should glance at it as he moves somehow gives it too momentum. 'Rere regardant.' He is looking for someone who may be watching him; his aloneness (and a connected sense of guilt) makes him turn and is in turning shattered. The obsolete, chivalric phrase is not pedantry (except in so far as Stephen is a pedant) but calls in forces that haunt Stephen, the medieval church and its philosophers. He looks back not merely into space but into time. And he catches sight of the ship, itself outmoded yet purposive and beautiful (Mr West suggests a connection between crosstrees and the Christian cross). And the ship isn't bound to him in any mystic way, though they are both 'homing', but is separate from him yet of the world of which he is a part. The superb sentence describing the movement of the ship gets its power from the integrated sense of motion (the present participles carrying the sentence along) plus the measure of controlled effort suggested in the words (particularly 'brailed up' and 'upstream'), the rightness of the rigging, the implication of successful, co-ordinated social effort, the human richness of 'homing' (also associated with the instinctive simplicity of a bird's movements). A contrast is made with previous descriptions of the casual movement of the weeds in the water 'To no end gathered; vainly then released, forth flowing, wending back . . .' and the indifferent, bobbing corpse of the drowned man, whose inquest is a worry to Bloom's friend McCoy.

The sense here illustrated of the interpenetration of human activity and experience is one of the great achievements of *Ulysses*. It emerges from Joyce's rejection of an individualist style of narrative, which sees the world merely from the point of view of the individual looking at it, and his powerful feeling for the interrelationships which go to make up society. As Alick West, in what seems to me the best short essay on *Ulysses*, has put it:

> In contrast to the traditional style, Joyce shows the individual action within the totality of relations existing at the moment. The traditional unity (of the nineteenth-century novel) is broken; in its place is the unity of Dublin.[12]

The most convenient example of this aspect of Joyce's technique is of course the tenth episode of *Ulysses*, the chapter which takes as its (rather obscure) Homeric parallel the episode of the Wandering Rocks.

This chapter, Mr Gilbert remarks, may in its structure and technique 'be regarded as a small-scale model of *Ulysses* as a whole'.[13] I think this is somewhat misleading, for the chapter is built on a far simpler plan than the book as a whole and does not include, even in embryo form, many of the themes which turn out to be the most important elements in its pattern; but it is nevertheless useful for the illustration of this particular quality of inter-relatedness.

The chapter consists of eighteen episodes—varying from a page to about six pages in length—which give the effect of a cross-section of life in the Dublin streets between three and four o'clock in the afternoon. Two of the episodes involve the principal characters of the novel, Bloom and Stephen, the remainder deal with the progress of other figures who take some part in other episodes in the book, the exception being the final section in which the Lord Lieutenant of Ireland makes his only appearance.

The whole of the chapter is, clearly, more significant than the sum of its parts. The episodes are linked together in a number of ways. Several of the people involved pass by and are conscious of certain static phenomena—the posters advertising the appearance in Dublin of Marie Kendall, charming soubrette, of Mr Eugene Stratton and of the evangelist proclaiming the coming of Elijah. Several of the particular characters meet one another or are conscious of the same person: Father Conmee notes the queenly mien of Mrs McGuiness at whose pawnbrokers' establishment much of the Dedalus home reposes; Dilly Dedalus, having got one and twopence out of her impossible father, meets her brother Stephen at a bookstall: a one-legged sailor is given a blessing by Father Conmee and money by a stout lady in the street and by Molly Bloom who throws a penny out of the window as she makes her toilet in preparation for Blazes Boylan's visit. The chapter is linked with time past by the appearance not only of the main characters but of casual unnamed individuals like the sandwich-board-men (who wend their way right through the book) and with time future by strands which will not of course be taken up till later in the book: the flushed young man whom Father Conmee sees emerging with his girl from a gap in the hedge will turn out to be a medical student named Vincent in the hospital scene; Stephen notices 'a sailorman, rust bearded' who will cross his path again in the cabman's shelter late at night.

Again, in the midst of a particular episode, one comes upon a sentence which has no apparent connection with the immediate scene but simply links it with another episode, giving the effect of the simultaneous activities going on in the city and reminding us that a character has not ceased to have his being just because he is not at that moment being described. In the middle of a discussion over tea about Stephen's view on *Hamlet* between Mulligan and Haines we are suddenly confronted with an apparently stray sentence about the one-legged sailor and the words '*England expects. . . .*' Here the effect is a little more complex than a mere reminder of the continued and apparently unrelated existence of the sailor moving down Nelson Street. It points the way towards the Lord Lieutenant and also serves to place Haines's views on Stephen, for Haines's part in the pattern of *Ulysses* is always that of the smug and small-souled representative of the alien imperial state.

The main purpose of the Wandering Rocks chapter is certainly the achievement on the surface level of a sense of the teeming life of Dublin and of a reality deeper than and independent of the individual consciousness. But the chapter is, necessarily, not merely objective documentary (and even a documentary is of course anyway selective); it also contributes continuously to the pattern of the total novel.

Thus the opening and closing episodes—Father Conmee and the 'viceroy'—besides contributing to the richness of the Dublin scene have a symbolic importance: they represent the Church and State which are the twin objects of Stephen's *non serviam* oath. In the course of the chapter our knowledge of both Bloom and Stephen is considerably deepened, not only through what they do but through other people's comments. There is, for instance, the splendid observation of Lenehan the journalist.

'He's a cultured all-round man, Bloom is,' he said seriously. 'He's not one of your common or garden . . . you . . . There's a touch of the artist about old Bloom.'[14]

And there is the poignant and beautifully controlled description of the encounter between Stephen and his sister Dilly.

Each episode in the chapter has its distinguishing rhythm and texture. The limitations of Father Conmee—his smugness, the urbane complacency of his inner heart—emerge out of every sentence of Joyce's prose. The quality of the prose of *The Sweets of Sin*, the pornographic novel Bloom buys in a bookshop, enters into the very essence of our knowledge of Bloom himself. The sudden move, when Stephen appears, to a more involved sentence-structure and a range of reference more erudite (not to say perverse) takes us without ado into Stephen's own consciousness. It is hard to say how objective Joyce is being when he gets to Stephen. Time and again the prose swings into a rich and luscious rhythm which one feels to be less 'poetic' and altogether more cloudy than is the intention. And yet in doubting the intention one is perhaps doing Joyce a serious injustice. By the end of *Ulysses* one has felt the full force of Buck Mulligan's exasperation: 'O an impossible person!' and I think one should rank this feeling as one of the real achievements of *Ulysses*. Just as Lawrence in *Sons and Lovers* succeeds despite himself in making us feel the intolerable qualities of Paul Morel so does Joyce here manage to 'place' Stephen. He is indeed 'Kinch, the loveliest mummer of them all'.[15]

Clearly it is impossible in a short chapter to discuss adequately a work of the complexity of *Ulysses*. Much of the material relevant to such a discussion has been gathered together in Stuart Gilbert's *James Joyce's 'Ulysses'*, a work of perhaps excessive piety but of an obvious value to the more-than-casual reader. Together with Harry Levin's lively and incisive *James Joyce*, Alick West's most perceptive essay in *Crisis and Criticism* and, on a more pedestrian level, Edmund Wilson's chapter in *Axel's Castle* (this essay is not really more than a starting-point), Mr Gilbert's book forms what might be described as a 'course of minimum reading' for the interested but not necessarily expert enquirer. I do not suggest that it is impossible to enjoy *Ulysses* without these critics any more than it is impossible to enjoy *Hamlet* without having read a word that has been written about it. But it is as foolish to insist that every work of art should be totally intelligible at a single reading or hearing as to make a deliberate cult of obscurity.

It is legitimate to criticise *Ulysses* on the grounds not of its complexity but of the nature of that complexity.

As has been said often enough it is an epic of disintegration, Odysseus and Telemachus meet only to drift apart again. The faithful Penelope lies dreaming of her illicit loves. Stephen, exiled by his own intellectual choice, and Bloom, a self-conscious though sociable member of an exiled race, are both in their different ways without roots, essentially lonely and—for all their social contacts— isolated. The intellectual life of Stephen, in whom thought and action have become separated and whose ratiocination is as sterile as it is ingenious, corresponds to the physical auto-erotism of the cuckold Bloom. The point of Buck Mulligan's obscene play for the mummers is equally relevant to all three of the principal characters.

The whole picture of Dublin which Joyce presents is of a society in hopeless disintegration extended between two masters— Catholic Church and British Empire—which exploit and ruin it. The family unit is as far decomposed as any other: there is a desperate weight of irony behind Dilly Dedalus's 'Our father who art not in heaven'. I do not think it is an exaggeration to say that throughout the book not one character performs a single action that is not fundamentally sterile. There is the odd kindness of course, the moment of compassion, the generous gesture. Bloom himself is, heaven knows, not a bad sort of chap. But there is a complete lack not only of any kind of human heroism but of any productive activity of any kind.

We see people eating, drinking, making love, arguing, they go after money, or they drift about; the churches and pubs fill and empty; and all this is felt happening simultaneously. But there is no sign of the productive activity without which none of this could happen. As a part of this organised production, there is not a worker in the book—at most an occasional cab-driver and a string of sandwich-board-men. We walk through the world meeting ourselves and we meet our relations and—so Stephen says—ostlers, but no industrial workers. . . . The reality of Joyce's social world is numberless acts of consuming, spending, enjoying of things that are already there. His selection of the social relations to be described is that of the consumer.[16]

The point of this criticism is not, of course, that Joyce ought to have written a different book, but that in the book as written there is something wrong.

Streets intersect, shops advertise, homes have party walls and fellow citizens depend upon the same water supply; but there is no co-operation between human beings. The individual stands motionless, like Odysseus becalmed in the doldrums.[17]

Joyce's failure to produce a great modern epic is closely bound up with his theory of the aesthetic 'stasis' and his personal sense of isolation and exile. In an important sense there is more of the essential feeling of the relationship of man to man and man to society in a great urban centre in the public-house ballad 'I belong to Glasgow' than there is in *Ulysses*. *Ulysses*, in its whole technical conception and in a thousand splendid flashes and insights, goes far beyond the negative individualism of *A Portrait of the Artist*. It is in many respects the most astonishing and brilliant attempt in the history of the novel to present man, the social being, in his full and staggering complexity. And it will always be read with enormous pleasure for its intimacy of insight and its phenomenal virtuosity. Yet the attempt flounders and not even heroically. The structure and basis of epic is replaced by a few tenuous and mystical threads which mean in the end almost nothing. The relationship between Bloom and Stephen, on which the whole pattern of the book depends, is a fraud, whose only significance is imposed from above by a vast apparatus of what can often only be described as verbal trickery. The tragedy of *Ulysses* is that Joyce's extraordinary powers, his prodigious sense of the possibilities of language, should be so deeply vitiated by the sterility of his vision of life.

More perhaps than any writer of English since Shakespeare Joyce was aware of the richness of content and significance behind the ambiguities of language and the literary possibilities involved in this realisation. But too often his exploitation of these ambiguities is an exploitation in the pejorative sense of the word. The ambiguous nature of language is its glory in so far as it expresses the actual complexity, the dialectical sense of growth and change which are at the very core of life and which a static, mechanistic, dead use of language cannot capture; but when ambiguity is not such an expression of reality but the mere artful juxtaposing of counters and the achievement of arbitrary effects then it is of course self-destructive. At least half the 'significances' of *Ulysses* are arbitrary significances which are, through their arbitrariness, given a kind of mystical haze. What *real* play is there to be made on the fact that Bloom's employer is named Keyes? What *real* significance is there in the inclusion of *La ci darem la mano* in Molly Bloom's programme or in the name of the typist Martha Clifford who is supposed via Martha and Mary to link up in some way with the Virgin? The case against the use of the association method run mad is not simply that it is arbitrary and confusing and indeed often leads to unintelligibility, but that it actually builds up a false web of associations, a pattern which, like so many of the patterns of modern psychology, has not the kind of basis in reality which it is held up to have.

It would of course be quite false to say that Joyce's achievement is totally vitiated by such weaknesses, important as they are. Laughter and compassion break through, turning virtuosity and pastiche into something far greater. Laughter is the greatest human positive of *Ulysses*, the assertion of sanity against which Stephen's isolation and Bloom's ineffectiveness break themselves. And along with the laughter there is a deep compassion, too, as in the passage when Stephen catches his sister Dilly buying a grammar to teach herself French. At such a moment Joyce's apparatus of leitmotif and cross-reference reaches into and extends the resources of language and we forget the jig-saws and the pedantry. Yet the total effect is unsatisfying.

What Joyce spends most care on is the formal side, watching that a phrase used on one page has the right echoes with phrases used on fifty other pages. But this sovereign importance of the verbal phrase is in contradiction to the life of the book. For it implies that the fabric is stable, and that its surface can be decorated with the most subtle intricacy, like the Book of Kells. . . . It assumes something as permanent as the church was for its monks. Yet Stephen and Bloom are both drawn as symbols of humanity in the eternal flux. On the other hand the sense of change in the book is so strong that this static formal decoration is felt to be a mechanism of defence against the change, and only valuable to Joyce as such defence. Joyce seems to play with the two styles of change and stability as he plays with his two chief characters. He plays with the contradictions; he does not resolve them. Where in Milton there is advancing movement, Joyce only shifts from one foot to the other, while he sinks deeper into the sand-flats.[18]

6

E. M. FORSTER: *A PASSAGE TO INDIA*

(1924)

E. M. Forster is not a writer of the stature of Lawrence or Joyce, but he is a fine and enduring artist and the only living British novelist who can be discussed without fatuity against the highest and the broadest standards.

Everyone who writes about E. M. Forster discusses liberalism, whether to insist (like Rose Macaulay and D. S. Savage) on the significance of his work as an expression of the liberal tradition or (like Lionel Trilling and Rex Warner) to doubt its total compatibility with that tradition. One of the difficulties in the discussion is that the parties to it all use the word liberalism with variations of meaning. One would prefer to dispense with the term altogether, yet Forster himself makes it hard to do so:

'I belong the the fag-end of Victorian liberalism. . . .'[1]

'(I am) an individualist and a liberal who has found liberalism crumbling beneath him and at first felt ashamed. Then, looking around, he decided there was no special reason for shame, since other people, whatever they felt, were equally insecure. And as for individualism—there seems no way of getting off this, even if one wanted to. . . .'[2]

'I am actually what my age and my upbringing have made me—a bourgeois who adheres to the British constitution, adheres to it rather than supports it, and the fact that this isn't dignified doesn't worry me.'[3]

The interesting thing, of course, about these statements—and even more about some of the sentences which surround them—is their objectivity, their remarkable consciousness of the historical implications involved. And it is this very consciousness which does in fact transcend liberalism even though it emerges from it and might be called in a sense its most extreme modification.

It is a dangerous game to try to pin E. M. Forster down. And yet such words as liberal, individualist, agnostic, certainly help, though I think they refer more usefully to his *attitudes* than to a more specific, coherent philosophy.

A Passage to India seems to me Forster's most successful novel. *Where Angels Fear to Tread* is perhaps not less successful, but is far less ambitious, while *Howards End* is quite as ambitious but the least satisfactory of the five novels.

The subject of *A Passage to India* is stated very clearly at the beginning of the second chapter, the first consisting entirely, and most economically, of backcloth. The two Moslems with whom Aziz is dining 'were discussing as to whether or not it is possible to be friends with an Englishman'. This is precisely what the novel is about and it is typical of Forster to make no bones about stating his theme.

The actual words of the statement are important. They are down-to-earth and they are precise. This is not to be a book about 'the problem of India' or anything so pretentious even though in the course of the exploration of the personal relationships at the core of the novel a great many deep, and indeed fundamental, social, political and moral problems arise. For Forster, despite all his emphasis on personal relationships, is far too sensible and far too worldly to attempt to abstract relationships from their actual contexts. A writer who can say of himself that he is what his age and upbringing have made him is unlikely to fall into the barren error of regarding a human personality as outside time and place.

And yet just as there is a subtle contradiction within Forster's attitude to himself—he who clings to a view of life which he sees clearly is basically not satisfactory*—so there is a subtle contradiction in his attitude to his characters. They are what their world has made them, yes, and they have, like their creator, a resilience, an almost insolent power of recuperation from the buffets and cruelties of life; yet they never quite manage to master life, even their odd particular corner of it, so that there is always a certain sense in an

---

* '. . . life has become less comfortable for the Victorian liberal, and . . . our outlook which seems to me admirable, has lost the basis of golden sovereigns upon which it originally rose. . . .'[4] How on earth can an outlook which has lost its basis be any longer admirable? How can anyone who has written of nineteenth-century liberalism 'In came the nice fat dividends, up rose the lofty thoughts'[5] ever take those thoughts quite at their face value again?

E. M. Forster novel of life's being rather more casual than it is, not flat, not mechanical, certainly not dull, but arbitrary somewhere deep down.

Up to a point this sense of the arbitrariness of existence is one of the great virtues of *A Passage to India*. The sudden shafts of violence, of horrors, of death and of the indifference of the living to the dead, are extremely effective in the novel, both in conveying the actual unexpectedness of life's detail and in counteracting the urbane, high comedy tone of Forster's narrative manner.

The central core of *A Passage to India* is the relationship of Aziz the Indian and Fielding the Englishman. The contrivances of the plot, often remarkably interesting and exciting in themselves, are important mainly as a way of illuminating this relationship and, so to speak, stretching it to its utmost. Both Aziz and Fielding are subjected to a strain so profound that their relationship can scarcely survive, even with all arbitrariness, all casual forms of misunderstanding removed, and the strain is the strain of the actual situation in which they exist, the strain of imperialism which, as in *Nostromo*, corrupts all it touches.

Because I have used the word casual in connection with *A Passage to India* it is necessary to stress the lack of casualness (in the Dickensian sense) in the actual construction of the novel. Every character, every theme and image contributes to the central pattern of the book. The precise establishing, for instance, of Miss Quested's character is essential not merely to make convincing her own actions in the story but to make clear the exact nature of the strains and problems she imposes on the Aziz–Fielding relationship. The description of the Hindu religious festival in the last section of the book is there not just to add colour and variety to the scene but to incorporate an essential element in the problem confronting Aziz and Fielding. Forster throughout the novel constantly uses religious themes and symbols not in the way of intellectual arguments but to deepen the sense of intangible forces involved. Aziz's sense of the past, his constant harping on the Mogul Emperors, is no mere personal idiosyncrasy but the expression of one of the many factors working upon the actual present situation.

Forster is immensely good at achieving in his novel the symbolic moment, the satisfying incident or episode which, though complete in itself, trembles with the more distant, more general repercussions which themselves thus force their way back into the book. A beautiful example is the little scene which ends Fielding's tea-party—an occasion pregnant with half-foreseen possibilities—

in his garden-house. The party consisting of the two English ladies, Mrs Moore and Miss Quested, the Moslem doctor, Aziz, and the Hindu professor, Godbole, is rudely broken up by Miss Quested's conventional Anglo-Indian sahib of a fiancé, Ronny Heaslop, who comes to drag the ladies away to watch some polo.

So the leave-taking began. Everyone was cross or wretched. It was as if irritation exuded from the very soil. Could one have been so petty on a Scotch moor or an Italian alp? Fielding wondered afterwards. There seemed no reserve of tranquillity to draw upon in India. Either none, or else tranquillity swallowed up everything, as it appeared to do for Professor Godbole. Here was Aziz all shoddy and odious, Mrs Moore and Miss Quested both silly, and he himself and Heaslop both decorous on the surface, but detestable really, and detesting each other.

'Good-bye, Mr Fielding, and thank you so much. . . . What lovely College buildings!'

'Good-bye, Mrs Moore.'

'Good-bye, Mr Fielding. Such an interesting afternoon. . . .'

'Good-bye, Miss Quested.'

'Good-bye, Dr Aziz.'

'Good-bye, Mrs Moore.'

'Good-bye, Dr Aziz.'

'Good-bye, Miss Quested.' He pumped her hand up and down to show that he felt at ease. 'You'll jolly jolly well not forget those caves, won't you? I'll fix the whole show up in a jiffy.'

'Thank you. . . .'

Inspired by the devil to a final effort, he added, 'What a shame you leave India so soon! Oh, do reconsider your decision, do stay.'

'Good-bye, Professor Godbole,' she continued, suddenly agitated. 'It's a shame we never heard you sing.'

'I may sing now,' he replied, and did.

His thin voice rose, and gave out one sound after another. At times there seemed rhythm, at times there was the illusion of a Western melody. But the ear, baffled repeatedly, soon lost any clue, and wandered in a maze of noises, none harsh or unpleasant, none intelligible. It was the song of an unknown bird. Only the servants understood it. They began to whisper to one another. The man who was gathering water chestnut came naked out of the tank, his lips parted with delight, disclosing his scarlet tongue. The sounds continued and ceased after a few moments as casually as they had begun—apparently half through a bar, and upon the sub-dominant.

'Thanks so much: what was that?' asked Fielding.

'I will explain in detail. It was a religious song. I placed myself in the position of a milkmaiden, I say to Shri Krishna, "Come! come to me only." The god refuses to come. I grow humble and say: "Do not come to me only. Multiply yourself into a hundred Krishnas, and let one go to each of my hundred companions, but one, O Lord of the Universe, come to me." He refuses to come. This is repeated several times. The song is composed in a raga appropriate to the present hour, which is the evening.'

'But He comes in some other song, I hope?' said Mrs Moore gently.

'Oh no, He refuses to come,' repeated Godbole, perhaps not understanding her question. 'I say to Him, Come, come, come, come, come, come. He neglects to come.'

Ronny's steps had died away, and there was a moment of absolute silence. No ripple disturbed the water, no leaf stirred.[6]

On the level of 'atmosphere' this is superb. With astonishing economy—scarcely anything has been in the Hardy way 'described'—the room, the tank, the garden, India is put before us, the strangeness to the Western people, Aziz's half-comic attempts to bridge the gap (emphasised by his false slang), the self-sufficiency of Godbole and his mythology, beautiful and ridiculous, all are richly conveyed and the figures of the servants in the garden, responding to the song, counteract any danger of the scene's becoming too obviously a mere symbolic dramatisation. Yet the symbolic quality is there, exemplified in something subtler than Ronny's failure to listen to the song. The song itself winds its way into the texture of the novel. 'I say to Him, Come, come, come, come, come, come. He neglects to come.'

He neglects to come throughout the novel. The atmosphere of *A Passage to India* is of a profound scepticism, tempered by a vague confidence which achieves no artistic expression commensurate with its importance in the overall tone of Forster's narrative. The negative side—the scepticism—comes over magnificently. Forster's refusal to be taken in by humbug, by the comforting commonplace, by the paraphernalia of dignity, gives to this novel its tang, its wonderful worldliness (Professor Trilling's insistent use of this word to describe Forster seems to me exactly right), its continuous tough delicacy of feeling.

Sir Gilbert, though not an enlightened man, held enlightened opinions. . . .[7]

On Aziz:

And unlocking a drawer, he took out his wife's photograph. He gazed at it, and tears spouted from his eyes. He thought, 'How unhappy I am!' But because he really was unhappy, another emotion soon mingled with his self-pity: he desired to remember his wife and could not. Why could he remember people whom he did not love? They were always so vivid to him, whereas the more he looked at this photograph the less he saw.[8]

On the Anglo-Indians' amateur dramatics:

They had tried to reproduce their own attitude to life upon the stage, and to dress up as the middle-class English people they actually were. Next year they would do *Quality Street* or *The Yeoman of the Guard*. Save for this annual incursion, they left literature alone. The men had no time for it, the women did nothing that they could not share with the men. Their ignorance of the Arts was notable, and they lost no opportunity of proclaiming it to one another; it was the Public school attitude; flourishing more vigorously than it can yet hope to do in England.[9]

Forster's urbane honesty, his infinitely sophisticated common sense, is at its very best in the precise placing of personal relationships. When Adela Quested comes to leave India and so must say good-bye to Fielding, at whose house she has been staying since the trial of Aziz, their relationship is brought not exactly to a climax, for there is no great intensity about it, but to the moment of assessment.

'Write to me when you get to England.'
'I shall, often. You have been excessively kind. Now that I'm going, I realise it. I wish I could do something for you in return, but I see you've all you want.'
'I think so,' he replied after a pause. 'I have never felt more happy and secure out here. I really do get on with Indians, and they do trust me. It's pleasant that I haven't had to resign my job. It's pleasant to be praised by an L.-G. Until the next earthquake I remain as I am.'
'Of course this death has been troubling me.'
'Aziz was so fond of her, too.'
'But it has made me remember that we must all die: all these personal relations we try to live by are temporary. I used to feel death selected people, it is a notion one gets from novels, because some of the characters are usually left talking at the end. Now "death spares no one" begins to be real.'
'Don't let it become too real, or you'll die yourself. That is the objection to meditating upon death. We are subdued to what we work in. I have felt the same temptation, and had to sheer off. I want to go on living a bit.'
'So do I.'
A friendliness, as of dwarfs shaking hands, was in the air. Both man and woman were at the height of their powers—sensible, honest, even

subtle. They spoke the same language, and held the same opinions, and the variety of age and sex did not divide them. Yet they were dissatisfied. When they agreed 'I want to go on living a bit', or 'I don't believe in God', the words were followed by a curious backwash as though the universe had displaced itself to fill up a tiny void, or as though they had seen their own gestures from an immense height—dwarfs talking, shaking hands and assuring each other that they stood on the same footing of insight. They did not think they were wrong, because as soon as honest people think they are wrong instability sets up. Not for them was an infinite goal behind the stars, and they never sought it. But wistfulness descended on them now, as on other occasions; the shadow of a shadow of a dream fell over their clear-cut interests, and objects never seen again seemed messages from another world.

'And I do like you so very much, if I may say so,' he affirmed.

'I'm glad, for I like you. Let's meet again.'

'We will, in England, if I ever take home leave.'

'But I suppose you're not likely to do that yet.'

'Quite a chance. I have a scheme on now as a matter of fact.'

'Oh, that would be very nice.'

So it petered out. . . .[10]

Relationships often peter out in Forster's novels, as they do in life, and as they never seem to, for instance, in Lawrence. The contrast between the two writers is an obvious yet an interesting one: Lawrence so intense, Forster so continuously relaxed. Is not the relaxation, the sceptical sophistication, likely to lead to a certain passivity? In a way I think it does. One cannot imagine one of Lawrence's characters lapsing into wistfulness (one wishes from time to time they would); but in Forster there is perhaps a little too much of it. The refusal to be heroic may be very human but it is also less than human. The relationship between Fielding and Aziz comes to grief—if that is not too strong a word—in the way such a relationship would very likely come to grief. On the personal level that is convincing enough. The doubt in one's mind lies in the attempt of Forster to generalise on the basis of that relationship. If the last paragraph of the novel means anything at all it means that the answer to Mahmoud Ali's original question 'whether or no it is possible to be friends with an Englishman?' is 'No, not yet, no, not there'. Not, that is, till the English have been driven out of India, when a friendship based on equality rather than imperialism will be possible. But might not friendship with Aziz have been possible had Fielding been prepared to go a little further, to renounce rather more than he was prepared to renounce of the imperialist attitude?

I think it is necessary to ask this question because Forster's failure to consider its possibility does something to his book. To attempt to sum up the final sense about life conveyed by *A Passage to India* one would have, I think, to turn towards some such phrases as 'Ah yes, it's all very difficult. There aren't any easy short cuts. Let's try and be sensible and honest and unsentimental. Above all let's be honest. And one day things will be a bit better no doubt.' It is, heaven knows, not an unsympathetic attitude, nor a valueless one, and it is a thousand times better than the defeatism to which, since *A Passage to India*, we have become accustomed. Yet it does, I suggest, reveal a limitation in the assessment of the capacity of human beings radically to change their consciousness. And this limitation reduces the book somehow, and all Forster's books. 'Donnish' someone has called him, 'spinsterish' someone else; 'soft' is the word he used himself. Inadequate words, yet one sees what they mean.

The truth is that in his determination to avoid any kind of humbug Forster tends to underplay certain of the underlying issues in life which often give rise to humbug but cannot be laughed away by its exposure. Keats's famous remark about being sure of nothing but the holiness of the heart's affections has a relevance to Forster. (It is one of those odd chances which one suspects to be more than chance that he should have named his chief English character as he did —another Fielding was the expounder of the values of the heart.) There is an important episode in which Ronny Heaslop puts the Anglo-Indian case to his mother, Mrs Moore:

'. . . I am out here to work, mind, to hold this wretched country by force. I'm not a missionary or a Labour member or a vague sentimental sympathetic literary man. I'm just a servant of the Government; it's the profession you wanted me to choose myself, and that's that. We're not pleasant in India, and we don't intend to be pleasant. We've something more important to do.'

He spoke sincerely. Every day he worked hard in the court trying to decide which of two untrue accounts was the less untrue, trying to dispense justice fearlessly, to protect the weak against the less weak, the incoherent against the plausible, surrounded by lies and flattery. That morning he had convicted a railway clerk of over-charging pilgrims for their tickets, and a Pathan of attempted rape. He expected no gratitude, no recognition for this, and both clerk and Pathan might appeal, bribe their witnesses more effectually in the interval, and get their sentences reversed. It was his duty. But he did expect sympathy from his own people, and except from newcomers he obtained it. He did think he ought not to be worried about 'Bridge Parties' when the day's work was over and he wanted to play tennis with his equals or rest his legs upon a long chair.

He spoke sincerely, but she could have wished with less gusto. How Ronny revelled in the drawbacks of his situation! How he did rub it in that he was not in India to behave pleasantly, and derived positive satisfaction therefrom! He reminded her of his public-schooldays. The traces of young-man humanitarianism had sloughed off, and he talked like an intelligent and embittered boy. His words without his voice might have impressed her, but when she heard the self-satisfied lilt of them, when she saw the mouth moving so complacently and competently beneath the little red nose, she felt, quite illogically that this was not the last word on India. One touch of regret—not the canny substitute but the true regret from the heart—would have made him a different man, and the British Empire a different institution.[11]

It is in the final sentence that Forster lets us down and exposes the weaknesses of his positive values. It is simply not true that one touch of genuine regret would have made the British Empire a different institution and it is this kind of inadequacy which gives rise to D. S. Savage's comment (in an essay which seems to me, by and large, very unjust) on *A Passage to India*.

. . . The ugly realities underlying the presence of the British in India are not even glanced at and the issues raised are handled as though they could be solved on the surface level of personal intercourse and individual behaviour.[12]

The reply to this is, of course, that Forster is writing a novel about personal intercourse and not a tract about the political situation; it is not an entirely convincing reply because Forster, by his own constant movement from the individual to the general, so clearly recognises that the two are subtly intertwined. It is, for instance, a weakness of the novelist and not merely of the social thinker, that one should constantly feel that Forster hates the public schools more than he hates what gives rise to them.

Another result of the unsatisfactoriness of Forster's positives is the element of mistiness involved in his treatment of Mrs Moore. It is difficult to isolate precisely this element. The presentation of Mrs Moore bristles with 'significance'. It is she who first makes contact with Aziz in the mosque. It is she who for some time appears to be bridging the gap between East and West. Then, in the first of the Marabar caves, she undergoes a psychic experience or vision— brought about by the dead, hostile echo of the cave—which destroys her sincere but rather tenuous Christianity but leaves her exhausted and passive. Although she believes Aziz to be innocent she allows herself to be sent away before she can testify on his behalf. On the Indian Ocean she dies; it has been for her a one-way passage.

Mrs Moore, living and dead, plays an important part in the novel. One cannot but associate her to some degree with Mrs Ramsay in *To the Lighthouse* and that other figure who so closely resembles Mrs Ramsay, Mrs Wilcox in *Howards End*. These women are all envisaged as somehow deep in the flux of things, associated with the processes of nature, at one in some profound intuitive way with the mysteries of the universe. They might be regarded, I think, as twentieth-century versions of the archetypal Mother.

Mrs Moore's vision is connected (partly through the image of the wasp which is significant both to her and Professor Godbole) with Hinduism, though it is hard to say just how. What the Mrs Moore–Hindu theme in *A Passage to India* really amounts to, I think, is an attempt by Forster, the liberal agnostic, to get beyond his own scepticism. There is a very interesting passage in which Fielding and Miss Quested, both individualists and sceptics, discuss how Mrs Moore could have known what happened to Miss Quested in the cave. The girl suggests the obvious 'scientific' explanation—telepathy.

The pert, meagre word fell to the ground. Telepathy? What an explanation! Better withdraw it, and Adela did so. She was at the end of her spiritual tether, and so was he. Were there worlds beyond which they could never touch, or did all that is possible enter their consciousness? They could not tell. They only realised that their outlook was more or less similar, and found in this a satisfaction. Perhaps life is a mystery, not a muddle; they could not tell. Perhaps the hundred Indias which fuss and squabble so tiresomely are one, and the universe they mirror is one. They had not the apparatus for judging.[13]

Is there not here Forster's own voice speaking? It is as though he is conscious at some level or other of the limitations of his own philosophy in which there is no room for a whole that is somehow greater than the sum of the parts and which constantly sidetracks his attempts at generalisation. The weakness of all Forster's novels lies in a failure to dramatise quite convincingly the positive values which he has to set against the destroyers of the morality of the heart. In *Howards End* he lapses into a rather half-hearted paean in praise of country life and the yeoman stock in whom lies Britain's hope. In *A Passage to India* the weakness lies in a certain vagueness surrounding the Mrs Moore–Professor Godbole material.

One might put it another way. Forster uses Mrs Moore and the Hindu theme to attempt to achieve a dimension of which he feels the necessity but for which his liberal agnosticism has no place. But because he is sceptical about the very material he is using he fails to give it that concrete artistic force which alone could make it play an effective part in the novel's pattern. Such passages as the twelfth chapter of the novel in which Hinduism is seen historically and a wonderful sense of age and mutability is achieved by 'placing' India geologically, are completely successful. But when Forster attempts to give to Mrs Moore a kind of significance which his own method has already undermined then the novel stumbles. The distinction between mystery and muddle itself becomes uneasy. The agnostic attempt to get the best of both worlds, to undermine mysticism without rejecting it, lies behind the difficulty.

And yet the tentativeness, the humility of Forster's attitude is not something to undervalue. The 'perhapses' that lie at the core of his novels, constantly pricking the facile generalisation, hinting at the unpredictable element in the most fully analysed relationship, cannot be brushed aside as mere liberal pusillanimity. He seems to me a writer of scrupulous intelligence, of tough and abiding insights, who has never been afraid of the big issues or the difficult ones and has scorned to hide his doubts and weaknesses behind a façade of wordiness and self-protective conformity. His very vulnerability is a kind of strength.

PART III

The Twentieth Century:
The Second Quarter

Aldous Huxley, *Point Counter Point* (1928)
Graham Greene, *The Heart of the Matter* (1948)
Joyce Cary, *Mister Johnson* (1939)
Ivy Compton-Burnett, *A Family and a Fortune* (1939)
Henry Green, *Party Going* (1939)

INTRODUCTION

The last twenty-five years have produced, so far as one can see at this close distance, no great new English novels nor indeed more than a handful of books about which one feels inclined to use the word good. There may of course be the undiscovered work of genius waiting to be unearthed. It may even be that future generations will discover in work which today we class as third-rate qualities we had not noticed or suspected. But it seems more likely that this will come to be seen by literary historians as a barren period, the novels of which will be read, if at all, as sociological curiosities rather than as living art.

The two qualities which strike one most, perhaps, as one surveys the period, are narrowness and pessimism. Both are, of course, quite understandable in their historical context, nor are they quite separable. The narrowness is to a considerable degree a by-product of the pessimism. Writers who feel unable to come to terms with the world at large tend to retreat into the only corner they can feel reasonably sure of—their own spiritual predicament and that of a few people like themselves. Hence the tendency of the twentieth-century middle-class writer either to turn in on himself and become entirely involved in his own neuroses or else to confine himself to an exceedingly narrow world in which he happens to feel at home. As a recent novel-reviewer put it:

Looking back on English fiction in the inter-war years, it is certainly fair to say that the best of it was almost entirely peripheral fiction, concerned with characters who in more classic writing would have been the 'bit players' rather than the heroes and heroines.[1]

Narrowness and pessimism: are they not, perhaps, mere words, expressive of what one reader happens to find unsympathetic? It seems to me that one cannot avoid the issue by such arguments. That the work of, say, Aldous Huxley, George Orwell, Arthur Koestler, Graham Greene and Evelyn Waugh is in its total effect pessimistic, that the picture of the human situation that emerges from the novels of these writers is in the last degree unhopeful and, as a result, unhelpful, is not a matter of mere opinion but is as clearly demonstrable as any statement of literary criticism can well be. The point is not merely that the material with which these writers are concerned is unsympathetic, that they write about a society which manifests all the classic aspects of decadence; what is significant is that the writers themselves partake overwhelmingly of the values of the society they depict. They are not simply writers describing decadence, they are decadent writers.

And why not? the question will be asked, what's wrong with pessimism and decadence? The simple answer, I think, is that such attitudes are life-denying and in consequence art-denying No one, of course, wishes to ignore the existence of misery and error, to deny that pessimism and decay are a part of human experience, to be reckoned with, not played down. No one wishes to deny that the experience of *Macbeth* is as valid and as important as that of *The Winter's Tale*; but the point is that whereas Shakespeare in *Macbeth* takes us with incomparable insight into the very toils of evil, allowing us no comforting escape from its reality, never does he capitulate to the sense that life itself is evil or meaningless, that man as a creature is inevitably doomed by his own inadequacies. It is Macbeth, not Scotland, that is damned.

Obviously it will not be easy to convince the reader who thinks that life is like a Graham Greene novel that Graham Greene is not a great novelist. The final appeal, as always, is to the world and the people in it. It is an appeal which, stated in so many words, tends to sound a little pretentious, like Mrs Ramsay's questionings about life. Yet it must lie behind all literary criticism that is not to become arid or sectarian.

ALDOUS HUXLEY

'Oh, wearisome condition of humanity . . .' begins the passage of Fulke Greville which Aldous Huxley uses as a prefix to his novel. And perhaps the first point to be made about *Point Counter Point* is that, despite its bulk and its pretension, it deals with extra-

ordinarily little of humanity. Far from offering a cross-section of
English society of the late 'twenties Huxley confines himself to two
groups which, significantly enough, interpenetrate in the world of
the novel: the upper-class group of titled Mayfair socialites and the
'literary' clique represented principally by Burlap, Rampion
(Lawrence) and Philip Quarles (who has many of the characteristics
of Huxley himself). It is one of the obvious weaknesses of the book
that although most of the personal relationships which bind it
together are tenuous enough, the Rampions cannot be brought into
the picture at all but spend almost the entire novel sitting in a Soho
restaurant to which selected members of the smart set repair from
time to time to listen to the (not quite convincing) voice of doom.
Hence, among other reasons, the justice of Lawrence's own complaint to Huxley that 'your Rampion is the most boring character
in the book—a gas-bag'.[2]

None of the characters in *Point Counter Point*, except the scientist
Lord Edward Tantamount and his assistant Illidge, does anything
throughout the novel except talk, engage in sexual activity, and
occasionally listen to music or write. Huxley is not interested even
in the trivialities of action among the well-to-do, and this makes
the 'social' scenes of *Point Counter Point*, like Lady Edward's
musical soirée, a great deal less vital as well as less amusing than
comparable scenes in Evelyn Waugh's *Decline and Fall*. Huxley
has little ability at characterisation and less at dialogue so that even a
simple comic set-piece such as the presentation of the fantastic Molly
d'Exergillod falls flat. Waugh does this kind of thing far better.

Point Counter Point is supposed to be the ruthless, not to say
scientific, anatomising of Huxley's world. Its fundamental artistic
weakness is that that world as a living organism never comes into
existence. It is as though Huxley is so keen to dissect that he cannot
first take the trouble to create. His novel entirely lacks the sense of
what makes the wheels go round in life. Even more than in the novels
of his spiritual (and technical) successor, Jean-Paul Sartre, life is
replaced by parasitism, a state of affairs tolerable only if the author
is himself fully aware of it.

Such vitality as *Point Counter Point* possesses is the vitality of a
sharp, if cynical, intelligence exercising itself on certain situations
and individuals which it has seen through rather than seen imaginatively. The Burlap sections of the book have this kind of 'life'
about them. Huxley has hit off Burlap, he has seen through the
utter pretentiousness and sentimentality of the man and presents
us with a vivid, malicious caricature. Similarly, he has seen through

the Walter Bidlake–Marjorie Carling relationship and can drag his
finger nail with perfect precision along the chipped edges of their
mutual exasperation. Most of the memorable sections of *Point
Counter Point* are the product either of malice or of masochism,
powerful emotions both but scarcely central enough to provide a
satisfactory standpoint for a view of the world. The masochism
reaches its most painful expression in the description of the death
of the Quarles's child. ' "It was a peculiarly gratuitous horror",'
Philip Quarles says of it. But not, perhaps, gratuitous enough. One
has the embarrassing sense of a personal inner compulsion behind
this episode which can only be described as pathological. Huxley
writes of Philip's feelings:

> He could not bear to let anyone come near his misery. It was private,
> secret, sacred. It hurt him to expose it, it made him feel ashamed.[3]

It is presumably for these reasons that the episode is introduced at
all. The 'gratuitous' horrors of Huxley's novels always seem to
have a double basis: in the first place they serve his own masochistic
needs, in the second they introduce a peculiarly bogus note of
dramatic irony. The death of the child in *Point Counter Point* is
linked with Elinor Quarles's decision to become Webley's mistress.
Why? Quite obviously Huxley does not believe or intend us to
believe that there is a divine retribution involved. Nor is he concerned to examine the effects of such a suspicion of retribution
(rightly or wrongly held) on Elinor Quarles herself. He is simply
exploiting the situation in a spirit of sadistic cynicism, calling in the
associations and ethics of *East Lynne* for purposes more subtle but
not less sentimental than Mrs Henry Wood's.

A good many of the characters of *Point Counter Point* do not
even have the two-dimensional vitality for Burlap and Beatrice
Gilray. Spandrell, for instance—a very central figure—is without
any kind of reality, a creation of abstract logic rather than of
flesh and blood. He is supposed, presumably, to represent the
ultimate in decadence, satanism minus glamour; one has only to
compare him with Dostoievsky's Kirillov in *The Possessed* to
reveal the shallowness of Huxley's cynicism. For all his determination to leave no horror unstated, to reach the extreme of
inhumanity, there is something very anaemic about Huxley's
decadents. They emerge not from a vision of the extremities of
human degradation but from a conscientious determination to
exploit a particular attitude. There is neither compassion nor indig-

nation behind *Point Counter Point*, the performance is nearer to a perverse, cerebral masturbation.

D. H. Lawrence, who liked Huxley personally (Huxley's introduction to Lawrence's *Letters* is an admirable one) wrote him a most interesting letter after he had read *Point Counter Point*:

> I have read *Point Counter Point* with a heart sinking through my boot-soles and a rising admiration. I do think you've shown the truth, perhaps the last truth, about you and your generation, with really fine courage. It seems to me it would take ten times the courage to write *P. Counter P.* that it took to write *Lady C.*: and if the public knew *what* it was reading, it would throw a hundred stones at you, to one at me. I do think that art has to reveal the palpitating moment or the state of man as it is. And I think you do that, terribly. But what a moment! and what a state! if you can only palpitate to murder, suicide, and rape, in their various degrees— and you state plainly that it is so—*caro*, however are we going to live through the days? Preparing still another murder, suicide, and rape? But it becomes of a phantasmal boredom and produces ultimately inertia, inertia, inertia and final atrophy of the feelings. Till, I suppose, comes a final super-war, and murder, suicide, rape sweeps away the vast bulk of mankind. It is as you say—intellectual appreciation does not amount to so much, it's what you thrill to. And if murder, suicide, rape is what you thrill to, and nothing else, then it's your destiny —you can't change it *mentally*. You live by what you thrill to, and there's the end of it. Still for all that it's a *perverse* courage which makes the man accept the slow suicide of inertia and sterility: the perverseness of a perverse child.[4]

I think Lawrence grants Huxley too much (I do not find in *Point Counter Point* the 'palpitating moment' of art; it has not the texture of art) and the business about destiny is something only the out-and-out Lawrentian could accept; but the essential truth about Huxley seems to me to be expressed here and expressed in the most relevant terms. It is no good trying to say what is wrong with *Point Counter Point* in terms of construction, style, characterisation and the technical weapons of literary analysis because what is wrong is wrong at the very heart. There is no respect for life in this novel and without such fundamental respect words curdle and art cannot come into being.

GRAHAM GREENE

Graham Greene is a far better as well as a more sympathetic writer than Aldous Huxley and there is a distinct sense of life in his novels. He is extremely good at conveying an atmosphere of unromantic corruption; 'seediness' is his forte and the colonial scene gives him a particular opportunity. He has mastered most of the slick techniques of the efficient film—especially the art of montage—and of the American novel of the 'twenties and 'thirties. His novels have a spare, taut quality which is very useful in counteracting their underlying pretentiousness. Graham Greene is never pompous.

The chief technical achievements of the American 'social-realist' novelists of the between-the-wars period were the perfecting of a very effective narrative style particularly suited to the conveying of a sense of physical action and the capturing of a tone of conversation at once colloquial and pointed. These writers were concerned above all to reflect the lives and sensibility of working people, of the common man as opposed to the refined one, to take the novel right out of the genteel atmosphere of middle-class living. It cannot be said that they were truly successful. What they tended to reflect was the sensibility not of the mass of the working class but of men and women on the periphery of that class—merchant seamen on leave, professional sportsmen, hoboes, conscripts, jail-birds, prostitutes, gangsters, bar-tenders, declassed intellectuals, students, bohemians, spivs and adventurers.

Graham Greene has inherited the experience of these writers: their narrative ease which takes violence and melodrama in its stride, their economy of construction (the complex folklore of industrial urban life taken very much for granted), a kind of brash sentimentality masquerading as toughness, an eye for the sharp detail, the sordid and the grotesque.*

How much of the manner of the Americans Graham Greene has absorbed may be seen from a snatch of dialogue at the climax of *The Heart of the Matter,* the scene in which Scobie says good-bye to his mistress, Helen Rolt (who played netball against Roedean):

He said, 'I came up here to say good-bye too. But there are things I can't do.'
'Don't talk, darling. I'm being good. Can't you see I'm being good? You don't have to go away from me—I'm going away from you. You won't ever know where to. I hope I won't be too much of a slut.'
'No,' he said, 'no.'
'Be quiet, darling. You are going to be all right. You'll see. You'll be able to clean up. You'll be a Catholic again—that's what you really want, isn't it, not a pack of women?'
'I want to stop giving pain,' he said.[5]

---

* I am thinking in particular of Ernest Hemingway, John Dos Passos, James T. Farrell and John Steinbeck.

This has precisely the tone and quality of an Ernest Hemingway conversation in *Fiesta* or *A Farewell to Arms*. It is also not far from the work of Michael Arlen, a now unread but once fashionable and daring novelist of the 'twenties.

The Heart of the Matter is a moral fable, a novel based on an abstract concept as to the nature of existence. The heart of the matter is the innate sinfulness of man and his need of divine mercy. Graham Greene's novel illustrates this concept.

The novel is set in a West African colony. In one of his travel-books Graham Greene suggests that there is some sort of significance in the geographical shape of Africa—the shape of a man's heart. The setting invites comparison too (perhaps unwisely) with another story of corruption and death, Conrad's *Heart of Darkness*, that extraordinary revelation of the horror of imperialism in the Belgian Congo. But there are other less pretentious reasons for the setting. The peculiarly sordid corruption of the colonial scene is bound to attract writers determined to spare no pains in the doing-down of the nobler human aspirations. There is a stock response here worth examining.

In a passage in *Point Counter Point* Elinor and Philip Quarles are being driven through the suburbs of Bombay when their driver runs over a dog:

> The sight of a dog running across the road just in front of the car aroused her from her reverie. How suddenly, how startlingly it had dashed into the narrow universe of the headlamps! It existed for a fraction of a second, desperately running, and was gone again into the darkness on the other side of the luminous world. Another dog was suddenly in its place pursuing.
> 'Oh!' cried Elinor. 'It'll be. . . .' The headlights swerved and swung straight again, there was a padded jolt, as though one of the wheels had passed over a stone; but the stone yelped. '. . . run over,' she concluded.
> 'It *has* been run over.'
> The Indian chauffeur looked round at them, grinning. They could see the flash of his teeth. 'Dog!' he said. He was proud of his English.
> 'Poor beast!' Elinor shuddered.
> 'It was his fault,' said Philip. 'He wasn't looking. That's what comes of running after the females of one's species.'[6]

In another of Huxley's novels, *Eyeless in Gaza*, in a well-known épisode a dog falls from an aeroplane on to the flat roof of a building bespattering sun-bathing lovers with its blood and guts. In *The Heart of the Matter*, when the despicable Wilson is on his way to a brothel he notes, from his car, that 'A dead pye-dog lay in the gutter with the rain running over its white swollen belly'.[7] Previously in the novel the same image has occurred in the midst of a key passage. Scobie, the principal character, is considering the corruption of the colony as he drives his car:

It was quite true. There was a retort in this colony to every accusation. There was always a blacker corruption elsewhere to be pointed at. The scandal-mongers of the secretariat fulfilled a useful purpose—they kept alive the idea that no one was to be trusted. That was better than complacence. Why, he wondered, *swerving the car to avoid a dead pye-dog*, do I love this place so much? Is it because here human nature hasn't had time to disguise itself? Nobody here could ever talk about a heaven on earth. Heaven remained rigidly in its proper place on the other side of death, and on this side flourished the injustices, the cruelties, the meannesses that elsewhere people so cleverly hushed up. Here you could love human beings nearly as God loved them, knowing the worst: you didn't love a pose, a pretty dress, a sentiment artfully assumed.[8]

When Wilson actually goes into the brothel, the comment is '... by entering this narrow plaster passage, he had shed every racial, social and individual trait, he had reduced himself to human nature'.[9]

The implications here scarcely need comment. The association of 'human nature' with 'the worst', especially the sexual worst, the linking of human sexual relationships with the activities of pariah-dogs, such associations are the stock-in-trade of a whole group of contemporary novelists. What one would note here is the glibness, not to say triteness, of the imagery. Men, ah yes, pariah-dogs. That will counteract any tendency for people to talk about a heaven on earth. One might suppose the considering of earth as heaven to be one of the commoner human failings. It is, of course, a characteristic of a certain kind of bad sentimental fiction. The question arises as to whether the sentimentality involved in seeing life as better than it really is, is necessarily more offensive than an opposite kind of sentimentality which takes pleasure in seeing the world as worse than it happens to be. The proverbial servant-girl for whom romantic fiction is said to be written does at least have understandable reasons for wishing her novels to be nicer than the truth; the desire for a fiction nastier than reality may well turn out on examination to have less respectable credentials.

On what grounds, beyond a general sense of disagreement with Graham Greene's view of the world, does one see *The Heart of* *the Matter* as a work of perverted sentimentality? Partly, I think, from the sense one has of a bag of tricks being brought into play. All the paraphernalia is here for a stock twentieth-century novel of corruption including the sense of the chief characters being caught up in a situation which they would not dream of trying to alter. Scobie *likes* the stink: the word 'love' is ostentatiously produced to make clear his attitude. Marlow, sailing up the Congo to penetrate the heart of darkness, is filled not only with horror, but with human indignation. True, Conrad somewhat muffles the horror in a certain wordiness which reflects the limitations of his powerful honesty,* but his total effect is one of vigour and moral insight. The death of Kurtz, exploited a little dishonestly by T. S. Eliot, is in no sense a symbol of the hollowness of man's nature, but rather a dreadful, ironic warning to his capacity to submit to evil, concretely associated in this case with colonial robbery.

In *The Heart of the Matter* one has, moreover, constantly the sense of the screw being turned, not in order to satisfy the developing needs of the novel as a work of art but in order to satisfy Graham Greene's abstract convictions. The whole thing, though extraordinarily slick, is too glib to stand up to any searching questions regarding its convincingness. Is not the dramatic irony altogether too insistent? That Scobie should embark on his journey into corruption through a series of events (starting from his need to comfort his wife for his failure to become commissioner) which would in fact have turned out differently from his expectations, this is convincing and legitimate play for irony. But that every single episode and turn of the story should have the same quality of deceptiveness is so unlikely as to defeat the purpose of the novel; the pattern, like that of a cheap bedroom wallpaper, becomes intolerable.

I am not arguing that a novelist should not, for the purposes of his artistic vision, choose and emphasise particular aspects of his material or that a literal probability is a necessary qualification for the eligible plot. No one would consider the story of *Romeo and Juliet* probable, but it has an inner justice and momentum of its own that is artistically convincing, partly because Shakespeare does not insist that his story is a symbol of life as such. He makes no claim to lay bare the heart of the matter. Whereas it is the pretentiousness of Greene's pattern that leads to his trying to put life into a strait-jacket.

* See above, p. 74 ff., and F. R. Leavis's discussion of *Heart of Darkness* in *The Great Tradition*.

Two examples will have to suffice. What artistic or human probability is there in the sacrificing of Ali, Scobie's servant, at the end of the book? That Scobie should at this point, whatever his suspicions or his corruption, hand over Ali to the mercies of Yussef, makes nonsense of the whole conception of Scobie on which the book is hinged. Clearly the episode is there, not from any artistic necessity, but for the sake of the over-riding pattern of the novel. If the relationship between Scobie and Ali were not to be destroyed something positive and humanly effective might emerge from the book and this must at all costs be avoided.

Then there is the trickery involved in the presentation of numerous characters, in particular Wilson, Ali, Yussef, Father Rank, the Portuguese Captain; Graham Greene does not play fair with his readers here. It is legitimate for a novelist who reveals his people through the consciousness of other characters to work by means of partial revelations, mistaken apprehensions and false tracks. The revelation of a human personality is, after all, a matter of almost infinite complexity. What is of doubtful legitimacy is for the novelist who takes an omniscient, God-like means of revealing his creations to give the reader a selection of facts which puts him at a special disadvantage. It is all very well for Henry James to keep us in the dark for most of *The Portrait of a Lady* about the facts of Madame Merle's career. Isabel herself is in the dark, and in any case by the end of the book the revelation is adequate for us to make our own judgements. In *The Heart of the Matter* Graham Greene deliberately keeps most of the *facts* dark, even to the end. Is Ali bribed? We don't know. Was the Portuguese captain a spy? We don't know. What about Yussef? Human relationships are tenuous, intangible, in flux, human beings have many sides; we cannot grumble at a novelist's failure to commit himself on such questions; it may well be the very intangibility that he is out to convey. But though motives may be obscure and contradictory, actions are less intangible; there are in life facts as well as doubts. It is Graham Greene's policy deliberately to play down facts and actions, to keep from his reader essential evidence which, though no doubt tricky and open to various interpretations, is, when all is said and done, the only thing we have to work on if we are to achieve morally responsible decisions and attitudes.

This is not fortuitous. It is an expression of a defeatism deep in Greene's philosophy which is in the end as life-destroying as Huxley's more vulgar cynicism. The 'moral' of *The Heart of the Matter* in terms of human action is that Scobie should have saved his own soul and left the non-Catholics to the mercy of God, which as Father Rank points out in the final chapter is more profound than Louise Scobie's. But Greene would obviously forestall criticisms as to the adequacy of such a summary by pointing out that, translated into terms of human action, an essential element of the moral discovery of the book is lost. The implication of *The Heart of the Matter* is that human action, as such, doesn't really matter much at all. The ethics and aspirations of sinful humanity are at best but poor things. It is the relation between man and God that is important. Without discussing the abstract truth or falsity of this proposition it is permissible for the reader to observe that it is one which unless discussed in terms of human action makes objective judgement (or indeed any kind of criticism that is not based on a supra-rational intuition) peculiarly difficult. If deficiencies in a way a work of art deals with reality are to be excused on the grounds that it is not, after all, reality that counts, then it is hard to see that any one critical statement is more relevant than another. We do not solve our problems by postulating life as the given basis within which art is relevant, but at least we make comprehensible statements possible.

The case against *The Heart of the Matter* is not that it fails to create a coherent impression or to involve much penetrating observation; the important criticism of it is that it reduces life by pressing it into a narrow mould. Graham Greene talks about Wilson in the brothel being 'reduced to human nature'. It is the way in which human nature in this novel is indeed reduced that constitutes its ultimate failure.

JOYCE CARY

Mister Johnson is also about Africa. Although published only a few years before *The Heart of the Matter* it belongs in subject-matter to an earlier era of colonial administration—the period, before the critical contemporary threats to the imperialist system as such, when Joyce Cary himself served as an administrator in Nigeria. That the exploration of the colonial scene should have played so important a part in the history of the British novel in the twentieth century is an interesting confirmation of the view* that good realist literature achieves its valuable symbolic quality by taking to their extreme points the underlying vital tensions of a particular social situation. The removal of the scene from London

* Discussed above, p. 97 ff.

to Africa or India or South America does not necessarily involve an escape from the central tensions of our own civilisation, on the contrary it may illuminate them.

Joyce Cary has played a comparatively lone game among contemporary novelists. Although he has experimented in a number of forms he has on the whole rejected the cults both of 'sensibility' (in the Virginia Woolf sense) and of pessimistic decadence (expressed generally through an obsessive introspection or through a rejection of humane values and potentialities). He is a vigorous and extrovert writer, not without the kind of sensitivity most admired by sophisticated readers—one recalls the beautiful novel of childhood, *A House of Children*—but capable of developing that sensitivity outward. One way of putting the problem which faces middle-class writers today is to say that they have a choice between refining their sensibility within the limits of a polite (i.e. middle-class) consciousness and tradition—the consequence of which is the production of a literature of limited relevance and vitality, and, incidentally, ends as anything but polite—or of moving towards a sensibility more inclusive, possibly less sophisticated, but more truly sensitive because coping more adequately with a larger sphere of the ultimately indivisible mass of human experience. The trouble with the middle-class sensibility is in the last analysis not that it is too sensitive but that it is sensitive to too little and therefore ultimately grossly insensitive. The inward-turning tendency of sensitive twentieth-century writers contrives to land them, in the long run, in a bog of *false* sensitivity.

Joyce Cary is a writer whose novels, though far from the 'tough guy' school of inverted sentimentality, have a kind of inner toughness most welcome and refreshing. Sometimes, as in *The Horse's Mouth* (in some respects his most important novel), the vitality seems to become a little forced, but the general effect is of a great and individual vigour. The attempt, in some of his books, to return to a picaresque approach—*Herself Surprised* is almost a twentieth-century *Moll Flanders*—is interesting. Here is a writer striving continuously to escape the polite tradition.

Mister Johnson has a sustained lyrical quality which arises from a quite remarkable unity of conception. Like several of Henry Green's novels it has something of the quality of a fairy tale; the world presented, though unmistakably related to the real world, has a self-consistency, a completeness, which beguiles the reader into an almost uncritical acceptance of its reality. When E. M. Forster writes about India we are all the time aware of an outside observer battling with problems which he may not—he is quite aware—fully understand: Joyce Cary's novel works in precisely the opposite way. Certainty is established. This *is* Nigeria, at any rate for the purposes of the book. The opening of *Mister Johnson* has the flavour of an objectivity which is almost that of the anthropologist. There are no ifs and buts about this writing.

The theme of *Mister Johnson* is the effect of the imposition of an alien code of morals and manners upon a native culture. Mister Johnson—the 'mister' is a title of social respectability—is a young African who becomes a Government clerk in an outpost in the Nigerian bush. He is a character of unbounded vitality, optimism and fecklessness. He is a 'big man', a civilised man, removed from and despising the pagan savages yet far more deeply one of them than he is one of the elect. He is an absurd figure with his patent shoes and total incomprehension of the civilisation he respects, deeply pathetic in his complete vulnerability, enormously sympathetic and amusing in his superb vitality and courage.

I do not see how within its appointed limits *Mister Johnson* could be better done. Humour and compassion are blended, not in the sentimental fashion of the following of an amusing scene by a pathetic one, but through the conveying at the same time of the pathos and the humour of the same situation, so that one laughs and cries at once.

A couple of examples of Joyce Cary's method will perhaps best indicate the nature of *Mister Johnson*'s success. This is a passage from near the beginning of the novel. Johnson, the clerk, has noticed with great satisfaction the girl Bamu who works a local ferry.

Two days later he finds her again in the ferry with her short cloth tucked up between her strong thighs. He gives her a threepenny piece instead of a penny; and she carefully puts it in her mouth before taking up the pole.

'Oh, Bamu, you are a foolish girl. You don't know how a Christian man lives. You don't know how nice it is to be a government lady.'

The dugout touches the bank, and Bamu strikes the pole into the mud to hold firm. Johnson gets up and balances himself awkwardly. Bamu stretches out her small hard hand and catches his fingers to guide him ashore. When he comes opposite her and the dugout ceases to tremble under him, he suddenly stops, laughs and kisses her. 'You are so beautiful you make me laugh.'

Bamu pays no attention whatever. She doesn't understand the kiss and supposes it to be some kind of foreign joke. But when Johnson tries to put his arms round her she steps quickly ashore and leaves him in the dugout, which drifts down the river, rocking violently. Johnson, terrified, sits down and grasps the sides with his hands. He shouts, 'Help! Help! I'm drowning!'

Bamu gives a loud, vibrating cry across the river; two men come dawdling out from a hut, gaze at Johnson, leisurely descend and launch another dugout. They pursue Johnson and bring him to land. Bamu, hidden in the bush, explains the situation in a series of loud, shrill cries. One of the boatmen, a tall, powerful man of about thirty, stands over Johnson and says, 'What did you want with my sister, stranger?'

'I want to marry her, of course. I'm clerk Johnson. I'm an important man, and rich. I'll pay you a large sum. What's your name?'

'My name is Aliu.'

The man scratches his ear and reflects deeply, frowning sideways at Johnson. He can't make out whether the boy is mad or only a stranger with unusual customs.

'It wouldn't do today,' he says at last.

'Why?'

Aliu makes no answer.

'When shall I come? How much money shall I bring?'

'Money? H'm. She's a good girl, that one.'

'Anything you like—ten pounds, twelve pounds.'

The two men are visibly startled. Their eyebrows go up. They gaze at Johnson with deep suspicion. These are high prices for girls in Fada.

'Fifteen pounds!' Johnson cries. 'She's worth it. I never saw such a girl.'

The two men, as if by one impulse, turn to their boat. As they push off, Bamu darts out of the bush and jumps amidships. Neither look at her. She sits down and gazes at Johnson with a blank stare. Aliu says over her shoulder, 'Another day, clerk.'

Bamu continues to stare. The two men give a powerful, impatient thrust which carries the dugout far across the water.

Johnson goes on shouting for some time, but no one can make out what he says. The village children come and stare. The general opinion is that he is mad. Finally, he disappears into the bush.[10]

The extraordinary vividness here is achieved by the absolute certainty of Joyce Cary's approach. Not a single doubt must creep in. We must not wonder: Would they really act like that? Isn't he perhaps being a little condescending? There must be no suggestion of ambiguity, except in so far as the actual relationship between Johnson and the bush people is ambiguous. What is aimed at is the security and confidence of a fairy tale or a scientific statement. Hence the absence of any adjectives which might imply a moral evaluation except from the inside of the scene. Objectivity could scarcely go farther.

But this does not mean that Joyce Cary's novel lacks a moral pre-occupation. Comment on the tragic situation is everywhere implicit. When, for instance, near the end of the novel Johnson, who has murdered the local storekeeper, is thrown into jail he finds there Saleh, the spoiled, effeminate boy who has been the Waziri's favourite but has now been superseded. Saleh immediately asks him for his shoes.

'But, Saleh, I need my shoes.'
'Need them—what good are they to you? In two days they will hang you. Oh, Johnson, do not be so cruel. I am only a boy. I am so unhappy. I can't bear this life. I cannot walk over the rough ground, and when I stumble, they beat me. You will give me your shoes now.'
Johnson is taken aback. He begins to reason with Saleh. 'But, Saleh, they are special shoes—the best English shoes.'
'Oh, how selfish you are. You are a brute.'
Johnson is moved. 'But, Saleh——'
'Yes, a heart of stone. You see me suffer here and care nothing.'
'But, Saleh, it is not so bad for you if you cheer up. Keep up your heart.'
'Oh, how cruel you are, Johnson. You don't understand what suffering is. You don't know how cruel people are. They say they love you, and they are nice to you, but suddenly they don't care at all. And then they betray you and beat you for nothing. You're as bad as the rest. You see me here dying of cold and misery without a friend.'
Tears come to Johnson's eyes from pure sympathy. 'But, Saleh, I am your friend, I am truly sorry for you. Here is my coat then—it will serve for a pillow.' He takes off his coat.
'I see you're going to put me off with rags and lies, like all the rest. You are cruel to me—and how selfish. What good will those shoes be when they hang you tomorrow. For it will be tomorrow, I promise you.'
'Well, damn it all, Saleh, here you are, then.' Johnson pulls off the shoes. Saleh seizes them and gives them to the pagan, who, smiling, rolls them up with the coat and puts them under his arm. Though he acts as Saleh's slave, his expression is full of the pleased curiosity of one who studies and enjoys new experience. Saleh then jerks the chain sharply, 'Get up, pagan.' The pagan rises quickly, taking care not to jerk his professor's leg-irons, and the couple jingle rapidly back to their own corner, where their loot is carefully rolled up in a mat.
Johnson sits looking at his bare feet for a long time, with an air of surprise. Then he says to his nearest neighbour with a voice inviting gossip, 'That boy, Saleh—fancy him being here.'

The neighbours, sitting on their heels against the wall, with their long thin arms hanging out over their knees, move only their eyes. They are a pair of cow Fulani, thin, dry and taciturn as only Fulani can be.

'A most surprising thing,' Johnson says in wonder. 'That boy was a most influential person—the Waziri's best friend—he had great power, and now, poor chap, well, you saw him. It makes you think, friends.'

The cow Fulani do not even move their eyes.

'It makes you think that a chap has to look out for himself—yes, you've got to be careful.'[11]

Here the tragic irony, though not perhaps very subtle, is extremely effective. It is not merely that Johnson's absurd generosity, his utter inability to distinguish between friend and enemy, is given a final illustration, the deepest irony lies in his own philosophical conclusion (it is one of the few moments when Johnson attempts to express his ideas about life). All that he can get out of what has happened to him is a 'moral' diametrically opposed to the truth.

The strength of *Mister Johnson* springs, I think, not only from Joyce Cary's firm and compassionate grasp of the nature of Johnson's tragedy but also from his remarkable insight into the function of myth among primitive peoples. Johnson is not merely a passive figure in this novel, the pathetic victim of imperialism and its by-products; he has a vitality of his own, potentialities of his own, expressed partly in his unfailing resourcefulness in playing the counters he does not understand but chiefly in his deep understanding of his own people and one-ness with them. The tragedy of Johnson the little clerk is pathetic enough; that of Johnson the poet-hero is far more profound.

This aspect of *Mister Johnson* recalls another remarkable work of art of this century, J. M. Synge's *The Playboy of the Western World*. The theme of *The Playboy* is that of the unheroic victim who has heroism thrust upon him through the needs of the people for a myth to enrich their barren lives. Christy Mahon, who murdered his da, becomes a living myth and thereby changes the lives of the people. And when the climax comes and he is exposed by the appearance of the father whom he is supposed to have murdered, the myth has done its work and changed him from a coward to a hero. The people lose their playboy but Christy finds himself.

Joyce Cary's use of the theme is, of course, different, but the emergence of Johnson as poet and myth-maker, organising and heightening the labour of the road-workers, shows an insight akin to Synge's. The relation between art and work in primitive society and the nature of tribal magic are brilliantly illuminated and in the terms not of the sociological text book but of a lyrical art.

There is, I think, an underlying weakness in *Mister Johnson*, a weakness most fully emerging in the final pages of the book when Johnson is shot by his hero the District Officer, Rudbeck. The limitations of Rudbeck and of the colonial administrators in general have been clearly expressed in the book. The final episode carries, in one sense, an appalling irony for it is clear that Rudbeck himself is totally unaware of the implications of what he has done. In the last sentence of the novel he is kidding himself into a day-dream version of the nightmare. Yet there is about these final pages an incomplete dissociation of the writer from Rudbeck's own sentimental attitudes. Rudbeck shoots Johnson as he would shoot a suffering dog to whom he feels a special responsibility and although the horror of this act is conveyed it is somewhat blunted by the underlying paternalism of Joyce Cary's own attitude. It is at this point that the lyrical approach wavers for we are forced now to evaluate the whole situation in terms more complex than the novel has hitherto demanded. Some rather fundamental questions begin to creep in. Is this an entirely just appreciation of the African situation? Does it not leave out something essential, that rising tide of African national consciousness and effectiveness which today one knows to be a vital element in the cultural and political issues of West Africa? Is not the whole novel conceived within a paternalist attitude—the attitude of the liberal imperialist—inadequate to the fullest and profoundest treatment of the subject? And is not the security, the confidence, the fairy-tale quality of the treatment based perhaps on a *false* confidence, an over-simplification?

I do not think these questionings affect the fundamental value and success of Joyce Cary's novel. It is a lyrical statement of a theme, not a sociological investigation, and its artistic vitality is in the end answer and justification enough.

IVY COMPTON-BURNETT

Miss Compton-Burnett is an extraordinarily accomplished and penetrating novelist of limited scope but unquestionable quality. The limitations are so obvious as to be scarcely worth emphasising. The subject-matter of all her novels is as closely related as their titles; she deals with genteel but declining upper-middle-class families at about the turn of this century. She has said, quite frankly,

that she has not been able sufficiently to come to terms with the
post-1914 world to feel that she can write about it:

'I do not feel that I have any real or organic knowledge of life later
than about 1910. I should not write of later times with enough grasp or
confidence. . . . And I have a dislike, which I cannot explain, of dealing
with modern machinery and inventions. When war casts its shadow, I
find that I recoil.'[12]

The statement exemplifies excellently Miss Compton-Burnett's
limitations and also her honesty. Her position is not unlike that of
E. M. Forster, except that one feels that she has made less effort to
overcome her blind spots. There is behind her bland acceptance of
her class limitations an element not of complacency but of defeat
and this gets into her books.

Some contemporary critics—and particularly Robert Liddell
whose essay is the best published appreciation of Miss Compton-
Burnett[13]—insist that this acceptance of rigid limitations is a positive strength. It seems to me rather a retreat that may be tactically
discreet but which nevertheless prevents Ivy Compton-Burnett,
like Henry Green, from being regarded as a major novelist.

The merits of *A Family and a Fortune* are very remarkable. Miss
Compton-Burnett is the wittiest of living writers and her wit, like
all true wit, is not a matter of superficial smartness or a cunning
ornamentation of style. It springs from deep in her observation of
life, from her critical consideration of the standards and values of
the society she is presenting.

'Well, of course, people are only human,' said Dudley to his brother.
. . 'But it really does not seem much for them to be.'[14]

The significant 'but' which throws ironically into relief the possible
contrasts in the word 'human', at once so much and little, the
minimum and maximum of man's potentialities, is typical of Miss
Compton-Burnett's method. So is the remark of Maria Swane:

'I like good people. . . . I never think people realise how well they
compare with the others.'[15]

Miss Compton-Burnett is sometimes compared with Jane
Austen and the comparison is not inept. Like Jane Austen she
examines with very little illusion and from a humane and critical

basis a limited society and the quality of her novels, like Jane Austen's, lies in their concrete revelation of human relationships and behaviour in very precise contexts. Like Jane Austen she is materialist and sceptical and like Jane Austen she eschews the generalised symbol. We are not offered a comment on the nature of life as such.

But *A Family and a Fortune*, as compared with *Emma*, is at once more critical and less positive. Jane Austen's world may have been, at the beginning of the nineteenth century, something of a back-water but it was a society with a good deal more future than that which a century later Miss Compton-Burnett anatomises. There is a confidence, a kind of radiance, in Jane Austen's writing which may have an element of complacency about it but also brings a vital sense of humane optimism which could scarcely penetrate to her successor. Miss Compton-Burnett's values, as they emerge in her novels, are humane and decent enough but there is little room for their expression in positive terms in the decaying country-houses from which her characters cannot or will not escape.

The very technique which Miss Compton-Burnett has developed is an expression of the disintegration which has taken place within bourgeois life and values in the course of a century. Her novels are built on dialogue—they contain the very minimum of descriptive writing—but it is dialogue of an original and highly convention-alised kind. Although she uses very subtly numerous voice inflexions (what a wealth of varied significance she can get from a 'Yes, dear' of Aunt Matty's!) the conversations in *A Family and a Fortune* are certainly nowhere near naturalistic, as Henry Green's are for instance. No one ever talked like the Gavestons and Seatons any more than anyone ever talked like Mirabell and Millament or the Macbeths. But like Congreve's or Shakespeare's Miss Compton-Burnett's dialogue is not so far removed from colloquial speech that she cannot use and echo the tones and rhythms of actual conver-sation. Her characters pretty obviously do not always say (out loud in the scene which the reader builds up in his imagination) the things they are made to 'say' any more than do the characters in Virginia Woolf's *The Waves*, in which 'Rhoda said' is a euphemism for 'Rhoda thought to this effect'. But whereas in *The Waves* the 'conversations' of the characters are undramatic, unrealised in the actual terms of a living, vibrating 'scene', in *A Family and a Fortune* the whole effect is one of a succession of dramatic episodes. The scenes are as firmly set in a particular place and time as Jane Austen's, who also bothers very little with descriptive backcloth.

What is new in Miss Compton-Burnett's novel is the continuous tension in the dialogue between what is actually said and what is expressed but only thought and the consequent ruthlessness in the exposure of the underlying issues and implications of a scene. Her conventionalised dialogue makes possible at the same time a sharpness of conflict, verbal, moral and psychological, of sometimes almost terrifying force and a fundamentally down-to-earth situation, unexaggerated in its essential qualities, which pins the conflict to reality and prevents the kind of abstraction which is the ruin of *The Waves*. Miss Compton-Burnett's method is essentially the method of the poetic dramatist (T. S. Eliot's dialogue in *The Family Reunion* is *technically* not at all unlike a Compton-Burnett novel, though not nearly so closely integrated); the significance and originality of that method is still, I think, generally underestimated.

It is not easy to quote from a book so closely woven as *A Family and a Fortune* for every point depends on what has gone before and no passage makes much sense out of context; yet it is necessary to try to give some illustration of the texture of Miss Compton-Burnett's novel. Dudley Gaveston, a middle-aged bachelor who lives with his brother's family, has inherited a fortune of two thousand a year, a fact which his brother's wife's sister, Matty, and her long-suffering companion Miss Griffin have just learned. Clement and Mark are Dudley's nephews, Justine his niece.

'Two thousand a year!' said Miss Griffin.
'Well, it is between a good many,' said Matty. 'It is so good when a family is one with itself. And you are all going to find it so.'
'To accept needs the truest generosity,' said Dudley. 'And I am not sure that they have it. I know that people always underrate their families, but I suspect that they only have the other kind.'
'It is that kind which is the first requirement,' said Clement.
'Clement, that remark might be misunderstood,' said Justine.
'Or understood,' said Mark.
'I don't think I should find any difficulty in accepting something I needed, from someone I loved. But I am such a fortunate person; I always have all I need.'
'There, what did I say?' said Dudley. 'An utter lack of true generosity.'[16]

The little episode is set off ∗y Miss Griffin's ingenuous exclamation of wonder. Matty's contribution (she is a female of the order of Goneril) immediately expresses—what the reader from his previous knowledge of her is anticipating—her determination to insinuate herself deep into the family circle at this important moment. It also reflects some of the labyrinthine insincerities upon which she works, for the family is in fact one with itself scarcely at all, only perhaps in its mistrust of her. Dudley's aphorism follows. It is both true and false, sincere and ironical. That there is a generosity involved in acceptance Miss Compton-Burnett wittily reminds us, but it is scarcely the principal issue in the reactions of the Gaveston family. Dudley's remarks reveal precisely the quality of his feeling towards the family, sincere and modest to the point of weakness, and at the same time ironical and realistic. What is 'the other kind'? It may be the kind of generosity involved in giving rather than receiving (the point Clement immediately takes up) or it may be a false as opposed to a true generosity. Both possibilities are relevant and indeed pointedly inter-connected.

Clement's remark (he is cynical and unsympathetic) again has the double function of revealing his personality and stating a relevant truth. Receiving is the other side of giving and dependent on it. The paradox of action into which the situation is moving is underlined by Mark's sardonic comment on Justine's bland remark, innocent (like Justine herself) in both the good and the bad sense— guiltless and unconscious. Justine who is good and stupid, bright, brave, infuriating, quite genuinely wants to smooth the situation, to interpret Clement's remark generously. Mark reveals in a word both the truth about Clement and the nature of Justine's automatic attempt to cover unpleasantness by a conventional phrase of agreed self-deception. We say we misunderstand when the truth is too unpleasant. And if we are like Justine we *do* misunderstand.

The next remark is not specifically given to anyone, though it is quickly apparent that it is Justine's. But I think the failure to put her name to it is quite deliberate, for the moment of doubt in which the reader is held has its point. Instinctively, we begin to apply the words to their possible speakers. It might be Aunt Matty speaking and in that case the first sentence would have an ironical undertone, for Matty loves no one but herself, and the second would be a deliberate tactic of false humility designed to impress on the family the superior fortune of their lot to hers. The fact that Justine's words might well be used with a different significance by Aunt Matty throws an immediate light on the natures of both, illuminating most subtly their different notes. And one of the points, of course, is that the illumination does not work wholly in Justine's favour. *She* can say with sincerity that she has all she needs, but the very posing of the statement in these trite terms leaves her open to our

criticism. A Compton-Burnett retort immediately suggests itself:
'Yes, my dear, but I never feel that that is quite enough.'

Dudley's rejoinder rounds the little exchange. It is both true
and ironical and although we know Dudley means it kindly, taking
Justine's remarks at their (and her) face value, it has a sting to it,
too. In *A Family and a Fortune* we are allowed to take nothing for
granted. Every easy convention, whether of action or speech, is
probed and questioned. Miss Compton-Burnett's dialectical method,
which exposes the horror as well as the triteness of the cliché, and
will never let us forget that there are two sides to every coin, is a
critical weapon of devastating effect.

It is hard to imagine a more uncompromising revelation than
A Family and a Fortune of the nature of the lives and values of
the declining well-to-do. Miss Compton-Burnett is almost entirely
without sentimentality, though a certain note of it perhaps creeps
into the conception of Aubrey, the backward child who sees more
of the truth than anyone else in the book. For all the artifice of the
technique it is an extremely worldly novel, making almost no concessions to our complacency. The wicked are not punished in
A Family and a Fortune, nor does experience mellow the impercep-
tive. Individuals and their relationships are stripped of pretence and
they quickly gather about them new pretences. Dudley Gaveston,
the most intelligent and humane of the novel's characters, is weighed
and found wanting. He sees more clearly than the rest what their
world is like, not in the sense that he makes any kind of generalised
analysis of the social situation, but in the sense that the nature of
the personal relationships (particularly with his brother) in which
he is involved becomes through his experiences clarified. It is
Dudley's tragedy that he sees at the end that he has played his
passive role of second fiddle too long to be able now to take any
other part; he is incapable of even trying effectively to change the
situation and capitulates in an ironic ending in which a pretence is
made, through Justine's imperceptiveness and the imagery of the
final sentence, that nothing has happened and even that something
has been gained. For her doomed characters Miss Compton-
Burnett has infinite understanding and a deep sympathy but not
one word of comfort. She makes us know them for what they
are.

Why, then, is the final effect of *A Family and a Fortune* not, like
that of *Point Counter Point* and *The Heart of the Matter*, totally
depressing and life-denying? I think there are two essential reasons.
In the first place Miss Compton-Burnett nowhere implies that the

situation she reveals is typical of all of life. Her novel is not a moral
fable, illustrating an allegedly absolute and universal truth. Therefore we see it as an illumination of a part of social life, not claiming
to be more. In the second place there is nothing unhealthy or perverse about the positive values implied in the writer's own standpoint. She does not offer us a vision of a decaying world as in some
sense attractive and desirable. On the contrary her controlled
intelligence and profound, deeply responsible wit increase our
critical awareness, sharpen our sensitiveness, undermine our complacencies. The total effect therefore upon the reader who to some
extent participates in the middle-class world and its values (and
which of us does not?) is the opposite of relaxing. There is an energy
behind Miss Compton-Burnett's wit which is exhilarating as well
as destructive. Her world may be one that is passing and indeed
almost dead, but so firmly is her experience of it grasped and defined
that we are the richer for sharing it.

HENRY GREEN

Henry Green is a novelist in the tradition of Virginia Woolf
though his subject-matter is very different from hers and also his
attitude towards it. *Party Going*, unlike *To the Lighthouse*, is a
comic novel, less pretentious than Mrs Woolf's, lighter in tone,
more critical in implication. Henry Green is not involved in his
subject-matter in the way Virginia Woolf is involved in hers and
the result is a kind of cool detachment which does not imply lack
of intimacy but permits a more sustained working of the critical
intelligence.

What is *Party Going* about? One answer would be that it is
about a group of rich and trivial young people who, on their way
to the south of France, get stranded for a few hours in a large
London railway terminus on account of the fog. An uninteresting
subject? The posing of the question in such terms indicates the unsatisfactoriness of discussing a novel of this kind in terms of what
it is *about* as opposed to what it *is*.

Of course the characters of Henry Green's novel are trivial. Of
course no one cares twopence whether they go to the south of
France or not. Of course it doesn't matter that they should be held
up by fog. Of course not one of them says anything intrinsically
interesting or important from the beginning of the book to the end.
If we are out for factual information or the abstract statement of
essential issues then we shall find enough and to spare in *Point*

Counter Point. But if all Huxley's encyclopaedic knowledge of facts
and all his awareness *on one level* of contemporary problems fail to
turn his novel into a living work of art, so does the triviality of the
subject-matter when abstracted from the novel fail to prevent *Party
Going* from bristling with life. The truth is that about a successful
work of art there is in an important sense nothing whatever to say.
Any discussion of what goes to make it up remains simply a discussion of what goes to make it up. To discuss the subject-matter
of *Party Going* instead of discussing *Party Going* is like trying to
say what it is about strawberries without mentioning their taste
(about which, too, in an important sense there is nothing whatever
to say).

The four young men and five young women who finally depart
for the Riviera do not share between them a single admirable
characteristic or emotion. Their lives are of an emptiness, of a horror
of futility, which surpasses casual description. But not Henry
Green's. He catches it. Evelyn Waugh who writes about these
people, doesn't. He makes them very different; because he is attracted
by them he makes them glamorous and witty and because he cannot
admit he is attracted by them he throws in a line of shrill indignation which is unconvincing.

Party Going is not a tract, it is an entertainment; but if a tract
were made out of it, it would be a tract, quite simply, on party-
going. In a way the most insistent and central character is one who
does not appear until the last few pages—Embassy Richard who
gate-crashed too many parties and was found out. But being found
out is only part of the game, too, and Richard joins the party to
France. His relations with them are no different from their relations
with one another, they do not like him less than they like each
other. Only Amabel who knows that Max is using Richard to keep
her occupied so that he can get going with Julia (with Angela Crevy
in reserve), tries to ward him off:

'But weren't you going anywhere?' Amabel said to Richard, only she
looked at Max.
'I can go where I was going afterwards,' he said to all of them and
smiled.[17]

The illumination of the title is complete. Party going where? Where
are any of them going? And yet going is the word. Moving somewhere and nowhere. The present participles of Henry Green's titles
are no more casual than anything else about his books. They reflect

his concern to catch things in motion, to see nothing as static, separate, ended, granted, abstract.

Henry Green is an extremely elusive writer. Like those strange birds which suddenly appear in his novels, he is poised and then swoops, touching an odd corner of experience, often tangentially. *Party Going* is full of a sense of the grotesque and casual within the highly organised and relatively rigid casing of social reality. No word as unbending as 'symbolic' quite fits *Party Going* ('Come off it', one of the servants would rightly say—colloquial tone perfectly caught); yet in this book the railway station with its mysterious entrance-tunnels and its 'huge vault of green' above is in a sense the social fabric. Within it life accumulates and is organised and there is a constant undercurrent of that productive activity which is the motive force of society and which so many contemporary novels lack. The absurd, dignified station-master, king of the place yet puppet of voices at the other end of a telephone wire, moves majestically through the crowd, prepared at a crisis, like a competent R.S.M., to rebuke the junior officer who is letting down his class. And within the station human life is divided. While the people wait for their trains under the great roof, the rich repair as a matter of course to the hotel and the richest take suites of rooms in which to wait and drink and bath and be in a position to fornicate.

It would be absurd to say that *Party Going* is about social struggle, but that is there too, caught in the casual, tangential way Henry Green uses to suggest big issues. Between the rich party, encased in the hotel, and the people in the station there is hostility and suspicion and fear. The rumour goes round that 'they' have broken into the hotel and there is a grotesque moment of silly panic. Very subtly Henry Green suggests the vulnerability of these people, their queer brittle quality, the product of their fatuous, empty, almost pathetic lives. When we reach the passage in the book most explicit in its evaluation of the whole situation it is given to one of the bright young things themselves and preceded by the statement 'Here he pointed his moral'. The fairy-tale element of the novel is stressed, the 'moral' removed from sententiousness and given a kind of absurd irrelevance. Yet the passage is not really casual, for more than any other it weaves together the themes and images of the book.

Here he pointed his moral. That is what it is to be rich, he thought, if you are held up, if you have to wait then you can do it after a bath in your dressing-gown and if you have to die then not as any bird tumbling dead from its branch down for the foxes, light and stiff, but here in bed, here inside, with doctors to tell you it is all right and with relations to ask if it hurts. Again, no standing, no being pressed together, no worry since it did not matter if one went or stayed, no fellow feeling, true, and once more sounds came up from outside to make him think they were singing, no community singing he said to himself, not that even if it did mean fellow feeling. And in this room as always, it seemed to him there was a sort of bond between the sexes and with these people no more than that, only dull antagonism otherwise. But not in this room he said to himself again, not with that awful central light, that desk at which no one had ever done more than pay bills or write their dentist, no, no, not here, not thus. Never again, he swore, but not aloud, never again in this world because it was too boring and he had done it so many times before.

It was all the fault of these girls. It had been such fun in old days when they had just gone and no one had minded what happened. They had been there to enjoy themselves and they had been friends but if you were girls and went on a party then it seemed to him you thought only of how you were doing, of how much it looked to others you were enjoying yourself and worse than that of how much whoever might be with you could give you reasons for enjoying it. Or, in other words, you competed with each other in how well you were doing well and doing well was getting off with the rich man in the party. Whoever he might be such treatment was bad for him. Max was not what he had been. No one could have people fighting over him and stay himself. It was not Amabel's fault, she was all right even if she did use him, it was these desperate inexperienced bitches, he thought, who never banded together but fought everyone and themselves and were like camels, they could go on for days without one sup of encouragement. Under their humps they had tanks of self-confidence so that they could cross any desert area of arid prickly pear without one compliment, or dewdrop as they called it in his family, to uphold them. So bad for the desert, he said to himself, developing his argument and this made him laugh aloud.[18]

'. . . if you have to die. . . .' The reference is to Miss Fellowes the aunt of one of the party-goers who has come to see her niece off and has been taken ill. No one is sure how ill, but whether she is going to die or not no one will mind, even though she has been put to bed in the hotel. Before being taken ill Miss Fellowes has picked up a dead pigeon which has fallen at her feet in the fog. This ambiguous bird, at once irrelevant and significant, wends its way through the whole novel.

The phrase 'no fellow-feeling' refers back to an incident in which one of the servants left with the luggage at the registration place, is kissed by a girl at whom he makes a pass, and reflects

'. . . it's fellow feeling, that's what I like about it. Without so much as
a by your leave when she sees someone hankering after a bit of comfort,
God bless 'er, she gives it him, not like some little bitches I could name,'
he darkly said, looking up and over to where their hotel room would
be.[19]

The contrast between the vague, incoherent, yet somehow
friendly unity of the crowd and the competitive bored antagonism
of the party-goers who call each other 'darling' but do not share
between them a generous emotion, permeates the book and is no
more accidental than the 'waste land' imagery towards the end of
Alex's ruminations.

The obvious criticism of *Party Going* is of the 'so what?' type.
Perhaps this novel does capture and illuminate most brilliantly this
social situation, this section of the human scene. But who cares?
Is it the function of good writing so to dispose? What do these
people matter? In what way are they worthy of the attention either
of writer or reader?

It is the old question 'Why read Jane Austen?' in a rather more
extreme form and again more than one answer is possible. The
straight reply 'because one enjoys it' is at once the best answer and
a question-begging one. In a sense it is the only answer, but it
avoids the two possible ramifications: '*Why* do you enjoy it?'
and 'Is your enjoyment perhaps a criticism of yourself?'

I would suggest that *Party Going* is a good novel because the
delight it evokes in the sympathetic reader comes ultimately from
an impression of life and its values which is vigorous and responsible
even though elusive and odd. The question as to whether many
people will in the long run find the novel very invigorating is a
different one. One cannot but feel that if those who enjoy literature
could discover novels whose scope and range was wider or—more
important perhaps—more central, they would not have a great
deal of time for *Party Going*.

It is not enough, in assessing the value of writers like Henry Green
and Ivy Compton-Burnett, to sum them up in some such phrase as
'good despite their limitations'. In so far as *Party Going* and *A
Family and a Fortune* are good novels, illuminating as art the area
of human existence which they treat, they need no apologies. In
getting straight one area of experience, however small, they help
by implication to get other areas straight. Life, like peace, is in the
last analysis indivisible.

What may, however, I think be legitimately said is that novels of the *kind* of Mr Green's and Miss Compton-Burnett's are not a sufficient response to the reasonable demands of the people in a democratic society for a vital and helpful literature. They are, it has to be said bluntly, middle-class novelists writing from a middle-class standpoint for middle-class readers. This is not to damn them nor indeed to fail to honour them for their integrity and talent. In a cultural situation in which no single writer has successfully solved the problems attending the production of a satisfactory popular fiction it would be ungenerous and unjust to criticise primarily those few novelists who within a particular sphere are doing respectable work. But it would be futile to pretend that the future of the English novel can lie along the directions they have explored. And, in the case of Henry Green, one has a sense of a certain perversity and even affectation in the novelist's insistence upon remaining on the fringes and in the odd corners of contemporary experience. Once the difficulty which the modern artist feels in coping with the central issues of a complex world is elevated into some kind of theory that defends the limitations of a minority culture as a positive virtue then the danger signal is pretty close at hand.

In the Preface to his book, *The Living Novel*, V. S. Pritchett excellently observes:

The forms of the novel are various, but it has enormously developed the field of its curiosity; new country has been subjugated in every generation; and the masters are those who have first invaded and liberated and added new territory. Let us admit that changes in style, method and belief often stand between us and the immediate enjoyment of many of the great novelists; but these barriers become unimportant when we perceive that the great are the great not only because of their inherent qualities, but because they were the writers who were most sensitive to the situation of their time. They are, in the finer sense, contemporary. I do not mean necessarily that they explicitly responded to external events, though they often did; evidently even bad writers reflect the age in which they live; I mean that the great are sensitive to an intrinsic situation. We say today that we are living in an age of transition, 'between two worlds'; the lesson of the master is that human life is always in transition; an essential part of his excellence is that he brings this clearly out in his work. We have only to glance at the second-rate novelists to see how they differ in this sense from the masters. The second-rate are rarely of their time. They are not on the tip of the wave. They are born out of date and out of touch and are rooted not in life but in literary convention.

The future of the English novel cannot be discussed in terms of mere literary convention. It is a problem bound up inextricably with the whole future, social and cultural, of the British people. The test of the future novelist, like that of his predecessors, will lie in the depth and sincerity of his response to the profoundest and most perilous issues of the time.

NOTES AND REFERENCES

N.B. Owing to the great variety of editions I have normally given chapter rather than page references in the case of novels which are divided into chapters.

PART I

THE PORTRAIT OF A LADY

1. R. P. Blackmur: Introduction to H. James, *The Art of the Novel* (1934), p. xii
2. *The Portrait of a Lady*, ch. III
3. ibid., ch. XXIV
4. ibid., Introduction (World Classics, ed.), p. ix
5. ibid., ch. I
6. ibid., ch. II
7. ibid., ch. IV
8. ibid., ch. V
9. ibid., ch. VI
10. ibid., ch. XVI
11. ibid., ch. VIII
12. ibid., ch. X
13. ibid., ch. X
14. ibid., ch. XVIII
15. ibid., ch. XLII
16. ibid., ch. LIV
17. ibid., ch. LIV
18. *Henry James, The Major Phase* (1946), p. 151
19. *The Portrait of a Lady*, ch. XLVII
20. ibid., ch. LV
21. ibid., ch. XIX

THE WAY OF ALL FLESH

1. *The Way of All Flesh*, ch. LXXXIV
2. ibid., ch. XXVI
3. ibid., ch. V
4. ibid., ch. VII
5. ibid., ch. XVIII
6. ibid., ch. XXII

7. ibid., ch. VII
8. *The Living Novel* (1946), p. 106
9. *The Way of All Flesh*, ch. LVII
10. ibid., ch. LXIX.
11. ibid., ch. LXVII

TESS OF THE D'URBERVILLES

1. *Tess*, ch. LI
2. ibid., ch. II
3. ibid., ch. III
4. ibid., ch. V
5. ibid., ch. VII
6. ibid., ch. XXXVI
7. ibid., ch. XXXV
8. ibid.
9. ibid., ch. LI
10. *English Studies* (1948), p. 19
11. *Tess*, ch. IV
12. op. cit., p. 6
13. *Tess*, ch. XXXV
14. ibid., ch. XX

PART II

NOSTROMO

1. *Under Western Eyes*, Pt. I, section III
2. *Abinger Harvest* (1946 ed.), p. 135
3. *Lord Jim*, ch. XXI
4. *Nostromo*, Pt. II, ch. V
5. ibid., chs. III, XIII
6. ibid., Pt. I, ch. VI
7. ibid., Pt. III, ch. I
8. ibid., Pt. III, ch. IV
9. ibid., Pt. III, ch. III
10. ibid., Pt. III, ch. XI
11. ibid., Pt. III, ch. XI
12. Letter to J. Bloch, 21 September 1890
13. *Nostromo*, Pt. III, ch IV
14. op. cit., p. 135
15. ibid., Pt. III, ch. IV
16. ibid., Pt. III, ch. XI
17. op. cit., p. 183
18. *Under Western Eyes*, Pt. I, section II
19. *A Personal Record*, Author's Note (1925 ed.)., p. ix
20. *Under Western Eyes*, Pt. IV, section I
21. *Nostromo*, Author's Note
22. ibid., Pt. III, ch. XIII

MR BENNETT AND MRS WOOLF

1. *The Common Reader* (First Series), (1948 ed.), p. 185 ff

2. David Cecil: *Hardy, the Novelist* (1943), p. 39
3. *The Art of Fiction* (1948 ed.), p. 189
4. Walter Allen: *Arnold Bennett* (1948), p. 44
5. *Aspects of the Novel* (1947 ed.), pp. 56–7.
6. op. cit., p. 65
7. op. cit., p. 192
8. *Tono-Bungay* (Penguin ed.), p. 9
9. Christopher Caudwell, *Studies in a Dying Culture* (1947 ed.), p. 80
10. op. cit., p. 350 ff
11. Quoted by J. Isaacs: *An Assessment of 20th Century Literature* (1951), p. 24
12. op. cit., p. 358
13. op. cit.
14. *A Treatise on the Novel* (1947), p. 125
15. *Phoenix* (1936), p. 547
16. ibid., p. 542
17. op. cit., p. 189
18. e.g. opening of section III
19. op. cit., p. 25
20. *Art* (1914), p. 44
21. op. cit., p. 93
22. *The Withered Branch* (1950), p. 95
23. David Daiches: *Virginia Woolf* (1945), p. 133
24. G. Lukàcs, *Studies in European Realism* (1950), p. 90
25. ibid., p. 91
26. ibid., p. 148
27. *To the Lighthouse* (Everyman ed.), p. 3

THE RAINBOW

1. *Phoenix*, p. 532
2. Anthony West: *D. H. Lawrence* (1951), p. 146
3. op. cit., p. 532
4. *Kangaroo* (1923), p. 171
5. *Letters* (1932), p. 198
6. *Penguin New Writing* (Autumn, 1946), p. 112
7. *The Rainbow*, ch. III
8. ibid.
9. V. de S. Pinto: *D. H. Lawrence, Prophet of the Midlands* (A Lecture, Nottingham) (1951)
10. *The Rainbow*, ch. I
11. ibid
12. ibid., ch. XV
13. ibid., ch. I
14. ibid., ch. VII
15. ibid., ch. XI
16. ibid
17. *Phoenix*, p. 537
18. *The Ambassadors*, Book V, ch. II
19. *The Rainbow*, ch. XV
20. ibid., ch. XVI

ULYSSES

1. *A Portrait of the Artist as a Young Man* (Travellers Lib. ed., 1932), p. 234 ff
2. *James Joyce* (1944), p. 74 ff
3. Stuart Gilbert, *James Joyce's 'Ulysses'* (1952 ed.), p. 204
4. op. cit., p. 281
5. ibid., p. 288
6. *Ulysses* (Odyssey Press ed., 1932), p. 23
7. ibid., p. 58
8. ibid., p. 560
9. Ibid., p. 581
10. op. cit., p. 73
11. *Ulysses*, p. 55
12. Alick West, *Crisis and Criticism* (1937), p. 165
13. op. cit., p. 225
14. *Ulysses*, p. 243
15. ibid., p. 7
16. *Crisis and Criticism*, p. 169
17. Harry Levin, op. cit., p. 96
18. *Crisis and Criticism*, p. 178

A PASSAGE TO INDIA

1. *Two Cheers for Democracy* (1951), p. 67
2. ibid., p. 85
3. *Abinger Harvest* (1940 ed.), p. 63
4. *Two Cheers for Democracy*, p. 68
5. ibid.
6. *A Passage to India*, ch. VII
7. ibid., ch. XXIX
8. ibid., ch. VI
9. ibid., ch. V
10. ibid., ch. XXIX
11. ibid., ch. V
12. *The Withered Branch*, p. 47
13. op. cit., ch. XXIX

PART III

1. Marghanita Laski in *The Observer*, 30 December 1951
2. *Letters*, p. 758
3. *Point Counter Point*, ch. XXXVI
4. op. cit., pp. 758–9
3. *Point Counter Point*, ch. XXXVI
5. *The Heart of the Matter*, Book III, Part II, ch. I
6. *Point Counter Point*, ch. VI
7. *The Heart of the Matter*, Book II, Pt. II, ch. I, section 4
8. ibid., Book I, Pt. I, ch. I, section 5 [My italics. A.K.]
9. ibid., Book II, Pt. II, ch. I, section 4
10. *Mister Johnson* (1947 ed.), p. 8 ff
11. ibid., p. 197 ff

12. *Orion*, a Miscellany (1945), A Conversation between I. Compton-Burnett and M. Jourdain.
13. In *A Treatise on the Novel* (1947)
14. *A Family and a Fortune* (Eyre & Spottiswoode; 1948 ed.), p. 54
15. ibid., p. 185
16. ibid., p. 125
17. *Party Going* (1947 ed.), p. 255
18. ibid., p. 195 ff
19. ibid., p. 162

READING LIST

There are many books about the English novel, including a large number published since this *Introduction* was written. The following suggestions for further reading make no claim to exhaustiveness.

(1) The largest, fullest, 'standard' work is:

BAKER, E. A.: *The History of the English Novel*, 9 vols (1924–38)

Almost any piece of information will be found here, including a long, now somewhat out-of-date reference list; but as a critical work it is uneven and uninspired. Of shorter 'histories' the best is

ALLEN, WALTER: *The English Novel* (first pub. 1954)

(2) Among less exhaustive general works the following may be found the most useful:

FORSTER, E. M.: *Aspects of the Novel* (1927)

An engaging and extremely readable book which raises more questions than it answers but will set the reader thinking.

LUBBOCK, PERCY: *The Craft of Fiction* (1921)

One of the first (and in many respects still the best) of the attempts to deal with some of the technical and artistic problems of the novel as a serious art-form.

LEAVIS, Q. D.: *Fiction and the Reading Public* (1939)

Despite its aggressive and sometimes infuriating tone this raises brilliantly a host of immensely suggestive critical and historical problems.

LEAVIS, F. R.: *The Great Tradition* (1948)

On George Eliot, James and Conrad this is, most people will agree, outstanding novel-criticism, serious, sustained and rigorous. The general line (especially of the first chapter), the conception of 'tradition' involved and the tone of much of the writing are more questionable.

JAMES, HENRY: *The Art of Fiction* (1948), *The Art of the Novel* (Collected Prefaces) ed. Blackmur (1934)

The great value of James's criticism is the opportunity it gives to see a highly intelligent and self-conscious novelist in action faced with the actual practical problems of his art.

LODGE, DAVID: *Language of Fiction* (1966)

Perhaps the most thorough and stimulating of recent exercises in novel-criticism.

ALLOTT, MIRIAM: *Novelists on the Novel* (1959)

Though the arrangement is a little odd this is a most useful book which brings together a great deal of interesting material otherwise widely scattered.

(3) Other general books include (alphabetically):

AUERBACH, E.: *Mimesis* (trans. 1953)
BURGUM, E. B.: *The Novel and the World's Dilemma* (1947)
CAUDWELL, CHRISTOPHER: *Studies in a Dying Culture* (1938) (Wells and Lawrence)
CHURCH, RICHARD: *Growth of the English Novel* (1951)
COX, C. B.: *The Free Spirit* (1963) (James, Forster, Woolf)
DAICHES, DAVID: *The Novel and the Modern World* (rev. 1960)
FOX, RALPH: *The Novel and the People* (1937)
GILLIE, CHRISTOPHER: *Character in English Literature* (1965)
GREGOR, IAN & NICHOLAS, BRIAN: *The Moral and the Story* (1962)
HARDY, BARBARA: *The Appropriate Form* (1964)
HARVEY, W. J.: *Character and the Novel* (1965)
HUMPHREY, R.: *Stream of Consciousness in the Modern Novel* (1954)
ISAACS, J.: *An Assessment of 20th Century Literature* (1951)
LAWRENCE, D. H.: Essays on the Novel in *Selected Literary Criticism* (1955)
LEAVIS, F. R.: *The Common Pursuit* (1952) (James, Lawrence, Forster)
LIDDELL, ROBERT: *A Treatise on the Novel* (1947)
    Some Principles of Fiction (1953)
LUKÀCS, GEORGE: *Studies in European Realism* (trans. Bone) (1950)
    The Historical Novel (trans., Mitchell) (1962)
    The Meaning of Contemporary Realism (trans. Mander) (1963)
MUIR, EDWIN: *The Structure of the Novel*
PRITCHETT, V. S.: *The Living Novel* (1946)
    Books in General (1953)
    The Working Novelist (1965)
SAVAGE, D. S.: *The Withered Branch* (1950)
SCHORER, M. (Ed.): *Modern British Fiction:* Essays in Criticism (1961)
SIMON, IRÈNE: *Formes du Roman Anglais de Dickens à Joyce* (1949)
STEWART, J. I. M.: *Eight Modern Writers* (1963)
TRILLING, LIONEL: *The Liberal Imagination* (1951)
VAN GHENT, DOROTHY: *The English Novel: Form and Function* (1953)
WEST, PAUL: *The Modern Novel* (1963)
WILSON, EDMUND: *Axel's Castle* (1931)
ZABEL, M. B.: *Craft and Character in Modern Fiction* (1957)

(4) On particular novels and novelists mentioned in this book: (N.B. In no case is anything approaching a bibliography of the particular author given, merely certain books that may be useful.)

MATTHIESSEN, F. O.: *Henry James, The Major Phase* (1946)

ANDERSON, QUENTIN: *The American Henry James* (1958)

KROOK, DOROTHEA: *The Ordeal of Consciousness in Henry James* (1962)

JEFFERSON, D. W.: *Henry James* (1960)
Henry James and the Modern Reader (1964)

STAFFORD, W. T. (Ed): *Perspectives on James's 'Portrait of a Lady'* (1967)

FURBANK, P. N.: *Samuel Butler* (1948)

COLE, G. D. H.: *Samuel Butler* (1949)

CECIL, DAVID: *Hardy the Novelist* (1943)

GUERARD, ALBERT J.: *Thomas Hardy, the Novels and Stories* (1949)

BROWN, DOUGLAS: *Thomas Hardy* (rev. 1961)

WING, GEORGE: *Hardy* (1964)

WEBER, CARL J.: *Hardy of Wessex* (rev. 1966)

HEWITT, D.: Conrad, *A Reassessment* (1952)

GUERARD, ALBERT J.: *Conrad the Novelist* (1958)

BAINES, JOCELYN: *Joseph Conrad* (1960)

ALLEN, WALTER: *Arnold Bennett* (1948)

NICHOLSON, NORMAN: *H. G. Wells* (1950)

KAGARLITSKI, J.: *Life and Thought of H. G. Wells* (1966)

DAICHES, DAVID: *Virginia Woolf* (1945)

LEAVIS, F. R.: *D. H. Lawrence, Novelist* (1955)

HOUGH, GRAHAM: *The Dark Sun* (1956)

VIVAS, ELISEO: *D. H. Lawrence, the Failure and Triumph of Art* (1961)

DALESKI, H. M.: *The Forked Flame* (1966)

BUDGEN, FRANK: *James Joyce and the Making of 'Ulysses'* (1934)

LEVIN, HARRY: *James Joyce* (1944)

GILBERT, STUART: *James Joyce's 'Ulysses'* (rev. 1952)

GOLDBERG, S. L.: *The Classical Temper* (1961)
Joyce (1962)

LITZ, A. W.: *Art of James Joyce* (rev. 1962)

BLAMIRES, HARRY: *The Bloomsday Book* (1966)

TRILLING, LIONEL: *E. M. Forster* (1944)

CREWS, FREDERICK C.: *E. M. Forster, The Perils of Humanism* (1962)

ALLOTT, KENNETH & FARRIS, MIRIAM: *The Art of Graham Greene* (1951)

MAHOOD, M. M.: *Joyce Cary's Africa* (1964)

BURKHART, CHARLES: *I. Compton-Burnett* (1965)

STOKES, EDWARD: *The Novels of Henry Green* (1959)

INDEX